MY LIFE AS A 50+ YEAR-OLD WHITE MALE

How A Mixed-Race Woman Stumbled Into Direct-Response Copywriting and Succeeded!

CARLINE ANGLADE-COLE

CLAC Publishing

Also by Carline Anglade-Cole

How to Write Kick-Butt Copy: Straight Talk from a Million-Dollar Copywriter

Anatomy of a Kick-Butt Control: How to Create a Winning Promo from Start to Finish!

Which One Won? How to Write Kick-Butt Headlines and Boost Response

How to Write FASTER Copy… Cut Down Your Writing Time By More Than 50%… and DOUBLE Your Income!

How to Write Magalogs, Tabloids and Other Monster Promos!

Available at www.carlinecole.com

Hardcover ISBN: 978-1-7352569-0-0

Paperback ISBN: 978-1-7352569-1-7

Ebook ISBN: 978-1-7352569-2-4

Audiobook ISBN: 978-1-7352569-3-1

This book was produced with the assistance of a remarkable writer and editor named Laura Gale. Feel free to contact Laura at laura.gale@lauraiswriting.com to help you develop your own book project.

Book cover design was courtesy of the one and only Rob Davis. Rob and I have worked together on dozens of direct-response designs. You can contact him at robdavisdesign1@comcast.net to help you with your design needs.

My apologies in advance for omissions, misspellings and perceived factual inaccuracies. I am recounting experiences and stories to the best of my quickly-fading memory.

"She's the best I've ever worked with!"

"Carline Anglade-Cole is without a doubt one of the finest copywriters I've ever had the pleasure to work with. She's extremely talented, fast and has an amazing number of controls to her name.

I've personally witnessed another well-respected business owner grovel and beg for a slot on her busy schedule. If you are ever fortunate enough to sign Carline up, you'll understand why. Definitely one of my favorite people to work with."

— Layne Lowery, President, Peak Pure & Natural

"A seasoned expert and creative genius!"

"Carline is, quite simply, one of the most brilliant copywriters I have ever known: a seasoned expert at creating direct mail packages and web pages that sell the bejeesus out of her clients' products.

Her unique perspective and red-hot sales copy have produced huge controls for major mailers from coast to coast. They literally beg to get on her dance card. I personally reserved every minute of writing time she'll give me! Take my advice: If you have the chance to work with Carline, JUMP at it!"

— Clayton Makepeace, Copywriter and Publisher

"Her copy is so hot... thank goodness she's married to a fireman!"

"It's not often a new writer is added to our 'go-to' arsenal, particularly as quickly as Carline was. We still miss having her as an employee, but the controls she's given us as a copywriter help temper our grief. We would hire her to write for us even if we didn't love her as much as we do."

— Erica Bullard, Senior Vice President of Business Development, Healthy Directions

"100% success rate so far!"

"We've had the pleasure of working with Carline on two projects in the last year. And she's got a 100% success rate so far! Both of her packages have been big winners for NatureCity. Even better, Carline is a pure delight to work with to build your business.

I look forward to every conversation with Carline, because by the time I hang up the phone, I know I'll have learned something that will immediately make our company more successful. And here's the good news for marketers... she's just getting warmed up! I have no doubt that her best packages have yet to be written."

— Carl Pradelli, President, NatureCity

"One of our best teachers!"

"Carline, I love having you as a regular in our Guest Expert Spotlight... you're really becoming one of the editors our readers can't wait to hear from again. And you put so much of your real-life experience into your themes.

Even though I'm sure our male readers love and learn from your articles, I think that many of our women readers really feel like you are talking to them... or even with them. I love reading your articles and I'm learning so much from them, too! Thanks so much!"

— Wendy Makepeace, General Manager, The Total Package™

"The uncrowned queen of controls!"

"Carline Anglade-Cole is the uncrowned queen of controls. Almost every time I go to my mailbox I get another one of Carline's promotion pieces. And most of the time, it's got some crazy headline that breaks all the rules... yet... it kicks butt in record numbers.

Carline is an absolute master of sales copy. And the work she has done so far for Biscayne Labs has been nothing short of sensational. Furthermore, she is a pleasure to work with and always... ALWAYS... a ton of fun on the phone. The truth is, I cannot wait... literally... for the third, fourth, fifth and sixth projects we work on together.

But I guess I'll have to wait. Getting on her schedule is no small feat. If you ever get the chance to work with Carline, count your lucky stars, you may have just hit the jackpot."

— Caleb O'Dowd, President, Biscayne Labs

"She produces 'to-die-for' results!"

"I can count on my fingers those who are true masters at copywriting. Carline is on that short list. I plan to hire her many times again and I hope you don't, because her waiting list is long enough as it is. She produces to-die-for results and to top it off, she's really cool too!"

— Sam Markowitz, President and Founder, The Sam Markowitz Group

"This woman delivers RESULTS!"

"What can I say about Carline Anglade-Cole? That she's in the rarified status of top A+ copywriters… that she's brilliant and creative and full of ideas… that she is a heck of a researcher — finding copy gems in the most arcane and dull scientific literature… that she is easy to deal with and delivers copy on time… yeah, I could say these things and more.

But you know what? While these attributes about Carline are true, there's primarily one thing a business owner, entrepreneur and marketer really wants… RESULTS! Carline delivers results!

Carline has for more than 20 years been my go-to copy-writer when I need to promote a nutritional supplement. She has brought in millions for me and for her other clients. Anyone wanting to learn the copywriting secrets of a world-class writer who thinks like a business owner and marketer needs to pay attention to what Carline has to say."

— Rick Popowitz, President and CEO, Biocentric Health

"Carline is more than my mentor…
she's my "Mr. Miyagi!"

"It blows my mind to see how Carline turns a basic thought into a killer control! It's no wonder she's an A-list, in-demand copywriter! She infuses her passion, insight and candidness in every package she writes. And that's only the tip of the iceberg for her! She's warm, kind-hearted, generous and a great listener! As her assistant, she's taught me some amazing copywriting techniques and very practical life skills.

Tapping into Carline's wisdom is priceless! She knows her stuff and she gives it to you straight. Only Carline can say it the way she does. And for those who really know her, you sense the love behind it. Her energy and passion are contagious! Once you get a taste of it… you're hooked! I'm grateful to have her as a mentor, friend and stellar boss! You rock Carline!"

— Cynthia Hill, Copywriter

"She's one swell gal!"

"I had the pleasure of working with Carline at Phillips Publishing in the 1990s, back when print newsletters were the thing. She was smart and an eager learner then. She is even smarter now, having mastered all the new forms of marketing. With her dynamic personality, she has been one of the most fun people I have known and also one of the most creative. In short, she's one swell gal!"

— David Franke, Former Group Editor, Phillips Publishing

"Helped me take my copy to the next level!"

"I've had the honor of working with Carline as my copy coach. And let me tell you, she's a master of emotion and storytelling that sells!

Carline grabs your attention with big ideas. Then she holds it with copy that feels like you're sitting across the table talking with her. You can't help but nod your head as you read along — and then take action. No wonder she's made millions for her clients!

On top of this, Carline is generous in sharing the strategies and techniques she uses to write million-dollar copy. You'll get it straight and to the point... just like you would from a best friend. She has helped me take my copy to the next level!

Now it's your turn. Apply the strategies you get in

this book. Then watch and see how it helps your clients — and you — make more money!"

— Chris Allsop, Copywriter

"An incredible teacher!"

"Carline is not only one of the most incredible people you will ever meet, nor is she just a gifted copywriter, she is an incredible teacher who spreads her knowledge far and wide.

From the first time I caught one of Carline's teachings, I was an instant groupie. When you get the pleasure of meeting her, she is just as warm and generous in person as she is online. Always a favorite on the AWAI stage, Carline just has IT, that intangible X factor. You feel it in her presence, you feel it from the stage and you feel it through her words."

— Jade Trueblood, Events Manager, AWAI

"One of the nicest copywriters and by far the youngest-looking grandma!"

"Carline Anglade-Cole is a great copywriter for three reasons. First, she has developed and honed her skills through years of writing winning packages. Second, she was mentored by the late Clayton Makepeace, arguably the best copywriter of his generation. Third, she cares about her work, her copy and getting great results for her clients, which she does on a regular basis.

Plus, Carline is one of the nicest copywriters

working today and also by far the youngest-looking grandma among us!"

— Bob Bly, A-List Copywriter

"Working with her is INSANE!"

"I have had the pleasure of getting acquainted in business with this "50+ Year-Old White Male" — and I can tell you, it is insane! Carline seems very nice, polite and even quiet at first glance… but once you let her jump into the business at hand, you will be overwhelmed by the intensity and depth of her thoughts and her direct and professional approach.

She has a clear mind, bursts out laughing all the time and she is extremely vivid. The queen of direct marketing! Carline the First!"

— Peter Kaminski, Dr. Hittich Gesundheits-Mittel

"Let me warn you now…"

"Carline is the only person I know who can teach you a huge lesson while making you almost pee your pants with laughter."

— Rebecca Matter, President, AWAI

"It's about time she wrote this book!"

"Carline's claim to fame is that she's one of the top copywriters in the world… but what I love about Carline — and I've known her for over 30 years — is that she is a lifelong learner. She has stayed true to her roots and her fundamentals and it's about time she wrote a book!

Her experiences and adventures in the world of copywriting and direct marketing needed to be documented and the way she has done so in *My Life as a 50+ Year-Old White Male* is astounding.

Her experience writing to 'grumpy old men' is a study in empathy, knowing her subject better than anyone and getting into the conversation going on in her prospect's head... on a level that no other grumpy old man could ever have done. And she did it as a vivacious, gleeful, very talented (and always youthful) woman.

I've seen some of the best marketers in the world be amazed by the way she writes and I think she's going to boost the careers of a lot of people in this business."

— Brian Kurtz, Founder, Titans Marketing and Author of *Overdeliver* and *The Advertising Solution*

"Her copy is memorable — if not infamous!"

"What I admire most about Carline is her integrity, openness and talent. From early on she has always lived true to her beliefs. She is very open and direct which is very helpful when collaborating with her on a project.

She also works quickly and makes her copy very real. I'll never forget her famous 'liver cleanse' package. It was not only a great read but the images of family members sharing their experiences were so amazing."

— Annette Payne, Owner, Measurable Results Marketing Agency

"I call Carline my SHERO!"

"No, it's not a typo — the 'S' is there because she is NOT a '50+ Year-Old White Male' but one of the most amazing women I know. I am blessed to know Carline as a friend, coworker, client and as a wonderful, generous, considerate, spiritual person.

She also helped me to get started with a new career as a freelance proofreader, researcher and English-German translator. Woohoo! Working with Carline — I can see why she is such a sought-after copywriter. This woman's schedule is always booked."

— Maria Charagh, Freelance Proofreader, Researcher and Translator

"So glad she's my MomBoss!"

"What can I say… Carline is a creative genius! The way her crazy, creative mind works is UNMATCHED when it comes to writing copy. Carline has branded her own unique style of writing that has no choice but to STAND OUT. She pours her genius into every single package she writes — and rolls out CONTROLS faster than any writer I've ever met.

But I would say Carline's greatest strength is her

overflowing generosity. Her willingness to teach and 'cheer on' up-and-coming writers reveals her amazing character.

If it wasn't for Carline's guidance, training and constant encouragement — I never would have launched my own freelance copywriting and graphic design business at age 19!

With Carline's mentorship, I got to experience the real FREEDOM that comes from living a writer's life — DECADES before most folks! Carline is hands-down a rare diamond — with many facets that make her a most valuable treasure.

I'm grateful to call her not only my mentor and friend, but also my Mother – and affectionately, 'Mom-Boss.' She's set the bar for the kind of writer and woman I always want to be."

— Tiara M. Cole, Copywriter and Designer, Crown Ink Designs

"Working with Carline is often a trip..."

"... A trip outside of my comfort zone. Her new and innovative ideas have led to much success and I'm grateful for the opportunities I've had to work with her. She's smart, kind, funny, super dedicated and makes every project an adventure... and that's what makes Carline Anglade-Cole one of my all-time favorite copy-writers."

— Gail Clanton, Healthy Directions

"She has the love and the guts to tell you like it is!"

"When Carline told me that she was going to write her story, I was over the moon. Not only is she one of the top copywriters in the world, she is also one of the most disciplined and prolific copywriters I know and she has the stacks of controls and the royalty war chest to prove it. Carline is an incredibly generous teacher and mentor. She's also one of the most energetic and passionate teachers you could hope to have. You'll never be bored and you'll laugh... a lot! Best of all, you can feel how much she wants you to succeed.

But what sets Carline apart from so many mentors is that she isn't afraid to have the tough conversations. If you're doing something that she feels is not in alignment with who you are, that might damage you or your reputation in any way, or isn't up to your own personal standard, she has the love and the guts to tell you. That is rare. I have been blessed with Carline's tough love in my career and I'm a better writer and mentor because of it."

— Marcella Allison, A-List Copywriter, Author of *Why Didn't Anybody Tell Me This Sh*t Before?* and Founder of the Titanides Mentoring Collective

"One of the people I respect the most in copywriting and the direct-response industry!"

"I've known Carline for nearly 30 years. We had a long history working together at Phillips Publishing and we both got into copywriting around the same time. She's been a wonderful friend and she's one of the people I respect the most in copywriting and the direct-response industry. She always steps up to teach, she's completely committed to writing kick-butt copy and if you ever have the opportunity to work with her or to learn from her, I highly recommend you grab it."

— Kim Krause Schwalm, A-List Copywriter and Copy Mentor

"If you want winners, you need Carline on your team!"

"I am here to tell you that if you want copy that works, you need to work with Carline Anglade-Cole. I've known Carline my entire career and she is a master. Not only will she give you great copy and winning controls, you will have fun doing it. There is no one else who will bring more energy and joy and life to your copy than Carline. If you want winners, you need her on your team."

— Cindy Butehorn, Owner, Net Effect Marketing

"I learn so much from reviewing her copy!"

"Carline has helped me a ton... reviewing her packages has been a tremendous help in my journey learning copywriting and in helping my clients with their copy-writing and compliance. If you are in alternative health and you need kick-butt copy, don't shoot yourself in the foot. You are so lucky to have Carline working in this industry. She is the best — hire her."

— David Jay, French marketer

**"You call her the Queen of Controls —
but I just call her Mom!"**

"It's true… she's a million-dollar copywriter who's broken all the rules of the game… and reinvented the wheel.

There's no denying she's a brilliant marketer with an eye for what works and what doesn't. And yep… she's a creative genius who's at the top of her game.

But to me… she's so much more. She's the woman who showed me by her own example how to raise four kids… run a copywriting business… and love what you do! She proved to me that with hard work and a lot of elbow grease — you can be happy mentally, physically and spiritually. She's a teacher, a friend and an awesome motivator.

She's my mom… and I couldn't have asked for a better one!"

— Milan Cole De Her, Copywriter, CopyMill Marketing

"A dream to work with."

"Carline is one of the most fun and joyful clients I've ever had the pleasure to work with. Her honesty, wit and whip-smart sense of humor kept me on my toes for the whole project — and I learned a heck of a lot from watching such an accomplished writer and business owner in action. I couldn't be more proud to have worked with Carline."

— Laura Gale, Ghostwriter

"So honored to have been one of her Copy Cubs!"

"Over a decade ago, I was lucky enough — some may say crazy enough — to be copy chiefed by Carline. I was just starting out and her unique ability to see how I wrote and what I wrote and to correct it effectively meant that I was then able to go out into the market-place and sell my skills. And I have to tell you that my income dramatically shot up because my skill level shot up from learning from an A-list copywriter like Carline. My advice to you — and the proof from my bank account — is to get with Carline as fast as you can so you can enjoy the benefit of her brain in YOUR brain!"

— Zac Romero, Copywriter

"Super energetic, very loving, very kind — a good person!"

"From the minute I met Carline, she made me feel really comfortable. She's really easy to talk to, super energetic, very loving, very kind — a good person. Her teaching is fantastic and always gets great feedback and if you're looking for someone to help you further in your business, Carline is your woman."

— Carla Zwaan, Titans Marketing

"A gifted copywriter, a great teacher and an inspiring human being!"

"Carline has the ability to cut to the heart of a problem and come up with a variety of potential solutions. She is able to take a group of people with varying skill levels and bring them to a common space of understanding.

Carline knows how to create and deliver value in whatever she does, professionally and personally. It has been a true pleasure working with her on various projects over the years."

— Denise Ford, Conference & Events Director, AWAI

Contents

MY LIFE AS A 50+ YEAR-OLD WHITE MALE

OLD WHITE MALE

How A Mixed-Race Woman Stumbled Into Direct-Response Copywriting and Succeeded!

CARLINE ANGLADE-COLE

It was a 50+ year-old white male who got my 20 year-old Haitian mother pregnant.

It was a 50+ year-old white male who taught me how to write copy.

It was the 50+ year-old white male market who provided me with the amazing and highly successful career that I wish to share with you now.

Could there be any better name for this book?

Dedication

I met Micarleo "Mickey" Cole the first day of high school in 1977 when we were 15 years old.

He's 18 days older than me — and he doesn't let me forget it. Mick has been an integral part of my life longer than everybody else — besides my mom.

One of the big reasons I'm still married to him is because he can always find a way to make me laugh. The first time it happened was when he responded seriously to a question in Mrs. Benson's tenth-grade English class — with two pencils stuck up his nose. And he's managed to make me laugh through good times... bad times... and even during childbirth.

For a while in high school, Mick was receiving 'love notes' unsigned by a secret admirer. He compared the handwriting of the notes to many possible suspects. But he never figured out who was sending them. What he didn't know back then was that I'm a 'forced righty.'

I'm naturally left-handed — but the nuns in my

Catholic school in Haiti viewed being left- handed as a 'sign of the devil.' So my left hand was literally tied behind my back and I was forced to write with my right hand. I became 'right-handed'— but only for writing. I'm still a lefty for everything else. I also developed a weird skill of writing backwards with my left hand. But that's a story for another day. Anyhoo...

... I say all this to confess: It was me who wrote all those love notes to Mick — with my left hand. I never told him that. Until now.

I got jokes too, Honey!

Mick is my rock. I anchor myself to him and that allows me to take on ridiculously crazy challenges and risks without fear. Mick loves me second — right after our God, Jehovah. And I treasure that rank order.

We started off 'so broke — we couldn't PAY attention.' He's helped me to remember our humble beginnings and that helps me keep the material gains we've experienced from copywriting in perspective. We were happy before copywriting success — and we will be happy long after copywriting disappears from our lives.

In our 37 years of marriage so far — my husband gave me four amazing gifts. We named them Milan, Tiara, Jael and Chadam. Nothing else he's ever given me — or vice-versa — comes close to these awesome gifts we call our children. However, I will say that our four grandsons — Dallas, Carson, Maverick and Colton — are very close seconds! And I thank my son-in-law Ethan De Her for these gifts also.

Mick always put his family's interest first. He put us

before job promotions during his 21-year career as a firefighter in Prince George's County, Maryland. He put us before personal pleasures and definitely before his own self-interest. He's a fierce protector and watchdog over our spiritual and physical lives — and for that, I am eternally grateful.

I love me some Mickey Cole.

* * *

The only other person I can say that I love as much as Mick is my mom Michelle "Mimi" Laroche Anglade. I was definitely not a planned pregnancy, but I am forever grateful that my mom didn't terminate her pregnancy — because you'd be reading a bunch of blank pages right now.

I'm going to talk about my mom a lot in this book. It's because she's taught me so much. Not necessarily with words — but definitely by her actions. My mom is a strong Haitian woman who was dealt a bad hand and turned it into aces. The many challenges in her life could've taken her out — but instead, she prevailed. And she did it with class and style.

I'm amazed at how my mom has been able to help so many family members. She's given them money — even though she wasn't wealthy. She provided long-term housing for numerous nieces, nephews and siblings, stayed up into the wee hours of the morning caring and comforting friends and family. I've got a dozen cousins who — down to this day — consider her their 'mom,' too.

She's 80 years old — and looks at least a decade younger. I hope I inherited those genes! She and my aunts Yolande, Maude, Jacqueline, Carole and my uncles Yves and Robert, came from an amazing mother — my grandmother, "Mama Da" — who passed away at the age of 99 on April 30, 2010. Again, I hope I inherited those genes.

My mom is the most unselfish person I know. She amazes me. The sacrifices she's made for me, my older sister Vivian and my younger brother Greg could fill a book much longer than this one. Yet she never complained. She's the ultimate 'Giving Tree.' If I could be half the mother to my kids as my mom was to me — I would be one heck of a mom!

Thank you Mom. I love you.

This book is for the two of you.

Foreword

C layton Makepeace was one of the biggest
personalities I've ever worked with — and
one of the most generous people I've ever
known.

I always told him if I ever wrote a book — I wanted
him to write the foreword. He agreed and said, "Get it
done." I even saved room in this book for him to share
his genius for storytelling and his insights on the world
of direct-response copywriting.

But I waited too long.

I started seriously working on this book on February
1, 2020.

Clayton passed away on March 24, 2020 at the age of
67 — right at the beginning of the COVID-19 pandemic
— from complications that may have been brought on
by the virus.

I regret my procrastination.

When Clayton came into my life, I was still in my

twenties, working as a marketing manager at Phillips Publishing. Clayton was one of the most successful copywriters in the industry. And now he was working with our Health Group to create sales copy to launch our products. I was nervous and excited that I would be in the same room with THE Clayton Makepeace.

When I get nervous, I usually say the first thing that comes out of my mouth. And I remember when I was introduced to him, I said, "With a name like Clayton Makepeace — I envisioned a tall Native American guy with a feather on your head, not a blond, blue-eyed teddy bear!" The room got eerily silent — and then Clayton busted out laughing and gave me a hug. Then he said, "I like your spunk." That was the beginning of our 30+ year relationship. During that time, he was my mentor, colleague and friend.

When I contemplated leaving Corporate America to try my hands at copywriting, I called Clayton for advice. He told me, "I can't encourage you to leave my biggest client — but WHEN you do — give me a call." That was just the little push I needed to give freelance copywriting a try. And true to his word — when I was officially on my own — Clayton set up the first meeting for me to meet one of his clients, Martin Weiss. That meeting led to many successful projects working with Clayton and Martin — and it gave me a tremendous amount of experience and confidence very early in my career.

Clayton was my mentor before he even knew it. I used to read all his copy. And when I needed to write sales copy at my job at Phillips — I would just ask myself, *"What would Clayton do?"* Then I would find some of his promotions and emulate his style.

When I became a freelancer and got to work with him on copywriting projects — I got to sit at the feet of the Master! And boy — he was tough. He told me to stop writing like a girl. When I protested and said, "I AM a girl!" He came right back at me and said — "But your market isn't! You're writing to 50+ year-old white males. Leave that girly stuff out!" He made me cry. But I soon realized that every time Clayton Makepeace made me cry — my income increased! So I welcomed the tears!

Clayton not only mentored me but he also took the time to mentor my two copywriter daughters, Milan and Tiara. He once gave Milan the courage to fire a bad client. When she took his advice — she found a better, more lucrative client almost instantly. And one of the very last projects he worked on was with Tiara for a new health book.

After Clayton passed, I started looking back over some old emails he sent me. One reason I'm not overly saddened by his death is because Clayton took the time to let me know how much he cared for me. He did that with everyone he loved. Even when he and I would argue about a project — he would "crack me upside the head with crits" (critiques) — but the conversations always ended with an "I love you." So without a doubt, Clayton made sure the people he loved knew it. But even still, when I found this email from him written a

few months before his death, I couldn't stop from
bawling...

> "YOU are one of the best things that has
> ever happened to me. You enrich my life
> in more ways than I can say. You are
> brilliant, hilarious and drop dead
> gorgeous. I revere your values. Every
> contact with you leaves me smiling and
> looking forward to the next time. In other
> words... I love ya!"

Now, a "Copywriting Papa" should never show
favoritism to his cubs — but Clayton sure did! He
always told me I was his favorite. And I loved it. It's
probably because I tried my best to be the "female
Clayton Makepeace." I won't say I succeeded. But I will
say it gave me a heck of a grand goal to aspire to!

Clayton was a master at pinpointing problems in
copy. And he never held back in letting me know how
to fix it. For example, a year before he passed, I asked
him for feedback on a pain-relief package that was
underperforming...

> "The copy isn't engaging enough to lower-
> level buyers... Are there unanswered
> objections? Is it credible? You could also
> consider a bigger discount with a
> deadline... more premiums, also tied to a
> deadline... Anything you can do to

intensify scarcity should get fence-sitters to take action.

And just a thought… Chances are a lot of your prospects are NOT in pain because they're on heavy-duty pain drugs (and those drugs, unlike your product, are covered by insurance).

Using this product could END the Opioid crisis in America. Look at the statistics — the carnage opioids are causing. Get some heart-rending stories.

Also: Doctors are reducing the amount of opioids they'll prescribe and pain patients are panicking. Tell them that pain is not the result of an opioid deficiency.

I also think that Reuben's story goes on way too long. I'm not interested in his pain, just my own. I would get it over with in a page or so, then address your prospect about his own pain."

Talk about feedback! He really THOUGHT about the positioning… the reader… what's currently happening in the marketplace. The crits were GOLD! And — oh yeah — I made those changes and turned the package from a dud to a stud! Ka-ching!

Clayton and I used to spend hours — even days — going over copy face-to-face. He showed me how nuances in copy can make a powerful impact on the subconscious minds of the prospect.

He challenged me to be BETTER every time.

I wouldn't be writing this book if it weren't for the lessons I learned from this '50+ year-old white male.' I am deeply indebted to him and so thankful that he knew without a doubt how special he was to me and my family.

Clayton leaves behind many loved ones. But there's one person in particular who deserves a special mention.

Wendy Marsh and I met Clayton on the same day. Yet our relationship with him took very different turns. Wendy was hired right out of high school by Phillip's vice-president, Bob King. She worked her way to the level of marketing director of our Health Group. When Clayton's launch package for Dr. Julian Whitaker's *Health & Healing* newsletter became a blockbuster success — Clayton became our Numero Uno copywriter. In fact — Clayton was actually paid a ridiculous amount of money NOT to work for our competitors. That's how vital he was to the success of our company.

Wendy and Clayton worked together closely and developed a personal relationship. She eventually left Phillips, moved to Florida, married Clayton and had two children, Katie and Justin. The Makepeaces also became a powerful marketing duo. Wendy never claimed to be a copywriter but she's an extremely good judge of copy.

I believe she was the silent force behind many of Clayton's successful promotions in the financial and health arena. "The Redhead" — as Clayton fondly called Wendy — has a knack for connecting with the prospect. So she had carte blanche to rip into Clayton's copy during the editing stage. Their creative collaboration was powerful.

I'm thankful for all the help Wendy has provided to me in my marketing career both at Phillips and as a freelance copywriter. I also tap into her copy savvy to crit my copy whenever she's available. She's provided remarkable insight that strengthened my copy and helped me hone in on the real issues facing my market. Thank you, Wendy.

Me with Clayton and Wendy at AWAI 2018
Bootcamp!

Introduction

My first opportunity to write a sales package was about... 'packages.'

Yep. I got my big break as a copywriter selling male potency products.

One morning in 1999, my phone rang. It was a list broker named Dave Nelson, from Walter Karl List Brokerage. Dave had a client who had just figured out his potency product buyers were mostly African American males. The client thought if he had a black copywriter, he would get better copy to target to his newfound market. So he asked Dave to find a black male copywriter to write the next package.

Well, back then, the direct-response industry was predominately middle-aged white men, writing packages and creating products for other middle-aged white men. When I hung out my shingle as a copywriter on January 1, 1999, I had only heard of one successful female copywriter — Barbara Harrison. I knew of one copywriter of

Asian background — Kent Komae. But that was about it. I didn't know ONE black copywriter — male or female!

The issue of color was very obvious to me, but the folks at the top of the direct-response industry seemed oblivious to it.

Just a few years earlier, when I was the senior marketing manager at Phillips Publishing, I was sitting in a meeting with the executives of the company. We were reviewing a new design called a 'magalog' that was hugely successful in the health industry. The magalog was a hybrid of a magazine and catalog. This format allowed us to add lots of color to our promotions. While the sales piece was indeed colorful — there were no PEOPLE of color in any of the pages!

So as we discussed this colorful piece — I mustered up the courage to ask, "Where are the people of color?" And the straight, no-holds barred answer I got was... "Carline, our market is a 50+ year-old white male."

Well EXCUSE me, but I knew for a fact that my African-American father-in-law was buying our products and so were his friends! So I thought the least we could do was TEST and let the market tell us if they wanted to see people of color or not.

But I was the only person of color in that room — and I was fighting an uphill battle. It's sad to think that just 25 years ago, diversity was still a foreign concept.

Now, I can understand the thinking. The direct-response health industry spawned from financial lists. And without a doubt — the vast majority of financial product buyers are 50+ year-old white males. So those are the folks who became the 'founding fathers' of the health market. However, I believed — and still do — that health transcends race. I'm not saying this because I'm smart... I just opened my eyes and SAW the people who were buying health products. And they were people of all colors!

So back to Dave's dilemma. He basically called me because he didn't know any black male copywriters — so he thought this mixed-race, female, wanna-be copywriter friend (moi!) was better than nothing! So you know what I did?

I fed the myth! I fueled the fire. I wanted to get that job! "Of course you need a black writer to tap into the black market!"

I couldn't believe I was actually saying that — and that Dave and the client believed me! Because I'll tell you this: even though I was just getting started in copywriting, I had worked with copywriters for many years. I knew the whole idea that a copywriter needed to 'be' the market was TOTALLY BOGUS.

You don't have to *be* the market, you have to *know* the market!

I had watched Clayton Makepeace in action for years at Philips Publishing and what he did was tap into the dominant emotion of his market. He dug deep and found out what was keeping his prospect up at night — and he used that intel to create a captivating message to nail the sale!

That first freelance project was over 20 years ago now… and I'm going to let you in on a little secret.

Ready?

Anyone can learn to write for any niche.

Heck — I've been writing as a 50+ year-old white male my entire copywriting career — and did you see the photo on the cover of this book? A 50+ year-old white male I am not! I'm a woman of color who started writing for this niche in her twenties!

Men have been writing sales copy for 'female issues,' like menopause, for decades. My friend, Bill Hebden — an amazing copywriter — held the record for having the most and the longest-running controls for *Essence Magazine*, the premier magazine "For Today's Black Woman" — for years!

Bill would joke with me and say HE was more 'today's black woman' than I was! And he was totally right! If I would have gone up against him — with his experience and pulse on that market — his copy would've spanked mine.

He told me that *Essence* had tried for many years to find black writers to beat his control. But he said:

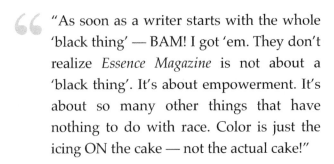

"As soon as a writer starts with the whole 'black thing' — BAM! I got 'em. They don't realize *Essence Magazine* is not about a 'black thing'. It's about empowerment. It's about so many other things that have nothing to do with race. Color is just the icing ON the cake — not the actual cake!"

Bill knew the women he was writing to. He didn't have to be the market — he knew his market! The fact that he was a 50+ year-old white male living in Philadelphia had nothing to do with it!

Clayton Makepeace knew it too. He wrote one of the most successful launches ever for Dr. Christiane Northrup's *Women's Health Letter* and got a 4% response. A number that high was unheard of back then! That package resonated with the female readers — and I can promise you that Clayton never had a hot flash!

By working closely with Clayton through the years, I really understood that writing great copy has nothing to do with sex or race or where you come from. It's about knowing your market and connecting with your reader! It's about saying, "I know and understand your fear — and I can help you."

So back to the male potency package...

(By the way — get used to me going back and forth with my stories. It's going to happen a lot! I love keeping my reader hanging on to find out what happened!)

... I convinced the client to give me a shot at beating his current control — which, by the way, was written by a 50+ year-old white male copywriter.

I asked Clayton to review my first draft — and his crit (critique) was simple and direct:

"You write like a [bleep] girl! Now go burp, fart and adjust your 'package,' and get into the mindset of your market!"

I was crushed — because I AM a girl! But I made the fatal mistake of losing sight of my market! These were guys, wanting stiff erections again! So I did most of what Clayton suggested and got into the mindset of my market. Then I went back to my computer — and here's the final copy for the lead Clayton helped me create…

 Dear Friend,

> *They say us guys are always in one of two modes: 1) Having sex, or 2) Thinking about having sex.*
>
> *Me? I plead guilty on both counts.*
>
> *The mere thought of a beautiful woman always got me excited. By the time I hit my 40s, I was well past the "amateur hour". I'd learned to savor a woman like a fine wine. For me, a sexless future would have been a fate worse than death… but then, the worst happened.*
>
> *On November 14, 1992, I went in for a routine medical exam. What the doctor said hit me like a ton of bricks: "John, there's a nodule on the left side of your prostate gland and the gland is hardened and abnormally enlarged. You have an extremely unhealthy prostate."*

Guess what?! That package BEAT the control — and gave me my FIRST winner! Woohoo! Now, I had a real sample to use to get more clients… and I was now making small royalties on my copy!

Let me tell you: Taking on that male potency project was scary. I didn't think I could understand the market. I was young. I wasn't a guy. My husband was no help — he said he'd never had issues in "that department." I was just desperate to get a shot at writing copy!

But I learned that desperation can be a good thing. That's why I think that if you're a writer, you should take on every challenge you can. Sometimes you'll hear someone say something like, "This package is for a more senior-level writer." Don't let that stop you. Fight for the job and fake it 'til you make it!

(And I'll tell you a bit more about how I quickly worked my way into bigger and better projects in Chapter Three.)

I believe a great idea can come from anybody... anywhere... any time. It's not only senior-level creative folks who have great ideas. If you come up with something new — go for it!

Don't be afraid to give clients something different and exciting compared to what they've been getting from other writers. Be willing to stick your neck out and the market will reward you for your guts!

That's how breakthroughs happen! Some of my best winners came from taking a risk. And you know what? Whether it works or not, you'll make a name for yourself in the industry as a creative risk-taker! Clients like that. Your name will get out and your business will grow.

That's why attending seminars is very valuable — key people who are hiring and who have great connections are going to be right there in one place! You get to meet them face-to-face. Get their contact info. That's how you get your foot in the door. And if you can't physically be in the room — go virtual! The COVID-19 pandemic taught us that virtual is the new normal! So try to attend webinars, live calls and online summits as often as you can.

I love the live events sponsored by American Writers and Artists, Inc. (AWAI), too. They can make a huge impact on your copywriting career. Katie Yeakle, Denise Ford and Rebecca Matter put on A-level seminars geared to help writers succeed in the direct-response marketplace. Get to know those folks!

Today, when I speak at AWAI — I love looking out at an audience of color! It's so great to see the industry changing in terms of both sex and ethnicity. There are lots of women in direct-response copywriting now and lots more people of color too. That's how it should be!

And no matter who you are, what matters is that you persevere and that you find a niche and style that works for you. I'm a mom, a wife, a woman. I'm an extrovert, a travel bug and a spiritually-minded person. And I think that using all these aspects of my personality is the key to my copywriting success — not what I look like or where I come from!

Now, before we really get into all the juicy stuff in the book, I've gotta warn you: This is not a book about the techniques of writing great copy.

If you want THAT info, my ebooks will teach you the practical skills that have helped me write hundreds of winning packages... and you can get 'em all on my website at www.carlinecole.com —

- *How to Write Kick-Butt Copy: Straight Talk from a Million-Dollar Copywriter*
- *Anatomy of a Kick-Butt Control: How to Create a Winning Promo from Start to Finish!*
- *Which One Won? How to Write Kick-Butt Headlines and Boost Response*
- *How to Write FASTER Copy... Cut Down Your Writing Time By More Than 50%... and DOUBLE Your Income!*
- *How to Write Magalogs, Tabloids and Other Monster Promos!*

You'll also find many of my current controls on my website. Study them. They're a great way to reverse-engineer how I put a winner together.

Now — THIS book is going to get all kinds of real. I'm sharing stuff I've never shared before. I think my journey may help you on yours... so I'm pulling the curtain WAY back. I want to help you see that no matter where you're coming from, where you're at now and no matter what you've got going on, you can build the life and career you dream about.

The first three chapters cover my early life — and the lessons I believe helped set me up for success, such as...

... Learning to hustle growing up in an immigrant family... meeting my husband... having my kids...

getting a foot in the door of the direct-response world... going from earning $8 an hour part-time — to becoming an A-list copywriter.

From Chapter Four onward, I'm going to share the biggest lessons I've learned along the way that made me successful. You're gonna learn how I built my business, one client at a time, how I work on my killer packages and how I keep my mind right and body tight! LOL!

And when we're talking about someone who is reading one of my packages, I'm going to refer to them as 'him' throughout this book — because I've spent my whole copywriting career writing specifically for the 50+ year-old white male market. But of course, all this applies no matter who your reader is or how they identify themselves. You can substitute in whatever is right for your market!

You're gonna learn a whole lot about copywriting by reading about my experiences — but do you know what I REALLY want you to learn from this book?

It's how to focus on what you want from your life... how to show up and put in the work to develop your own superpowers — so YOU can achieve your dreams!

Once you've read this book — I want you to truly believe, deep down in your gut, that you can overcome the status quo.

I want you to trust that if you work smart, take risks and stick to your priorities — you'll end up with a better life than you can even imagine right now.

This book is the legacy I want to leave for my family

and for the new generation of copywriters evolving right now. So I'm going to share everything I can to help you succeed!

I CAN'T WAIT for us to get started on this journey. And I want this to be a two-way conversation. So even after you finish reading the book — we can keep in touch. Just sign up for my CopyStar e-zine. It's free — and will help you continue to hone your copywriting skills on a regular basis. Just go to my website — www.carlinecole.com — and sign up.

Now — what are you waiting for? LET'S GO!

ONE

Crunch, Crunch, Crunch

O n November 2, 1967, I came to the United States from Haiti at the age of 6.

I was a pudgy kid with a roly-poly belly. And that was a good thing, because if you're a fat kid in Haiti, it means your parents can afford food.

Carline at 5 years old

My sister Vivian is four years older than me. She, on the other hand, was a bean pole. So when we landed at

Washington National Airport, standing next to each other, we looked like the number 10.

We had been waiting two years for this reunion. My mom, Michelle Laroche, had married Gerard "Gerry" Louis Anglade, when I was 4 years old and Viv was 8. Gerry got a job working at the Ugandan Embassy in the United States as a chauffeur. So right after their wedding, they moved to Washington, D.C., leaving me and Viv in the care of our grandmother, Mama Da.

In those days, people dressed up to travel. So, Mama Da made us these puffy, short-sleeved dresses so we would look nice. But after she finished sewing them, she remembered Mom had said it was "cold" in America.

Now, Mama Da had lived her whole life up to that point in Haiti. She had a tropical island mentality about cold… and the cold in Haiti is NOT the same as the cold in D.C. in November!

We didn't have coats — so once we got dressed in those short, puffy dresses, ankle socks and patent leather shoes — Mama Da gave us some 'insulation.' She scrunched up some newspaper and shoved it under our dresses so we would be warm!

Well, that newspaper crunched, loudly, with every step we took. We were crunching all the way through the airport! Crunch, crunch, crunch on the plane. Going up the escalators, crunch, crunch, crunch.

And when we got off the plane, we were crunching AND freezing! Thank goodness my mom showed up with winter coats for us!

That was my first experience with travel. It was so exciting. That big plane took me to a whole new world. A few hours on that plane changed my life forever… I loved flying. I was fascinated by the whole experience, even if it was embarrassing to sound so crunchy the whole time! That very first trip gave me a love of travel that has never gone away.

Haitian Women Know How To Hustle!

When I arrived in the US, I didn't speak a word of English. My native language is Haitian Creole and I was also learning French in school. My mom was so worried that Viv and I would fall behind in school that she encouraged us to speak only English. That was a big mistake! When us kids — which also included my baby brother Greg — learned English, that's all we wanted to speak. We surpassed Mom in learning the language — even though she had a two year head-start.

My mom eventually learned to speak English when she worked as a maid. Her employer was a Swedish woman named Mrs. Maane. I never understood why Mrs. Maane hired my mom. Neither one of them spoke English. The two of them would sit next to each other watching soap operas — trying to repeat the phrases they were hearing. Those 'English' classes forged a friendship between them that lasted over 40 years.

Life in the US was not easy for my family. Even though Gerry had a job as a chauffeur at the embassy, my mom had to take whatever work she could get so they could make ends meet. They lived in a rented room and tried to save up the money to send for me and my sister.

So, Mom always had two, sometimes three jobs. Oftentimes she worked as a maid, a cashier at a grocery store and a cafeteria server. I saw how hard she worked and how highly her employers thought of her. Her work ethic had a very powerful impact on me.

Mom always told me that she and Gerry didn't struggle to make a better life for us just to let us waste the opportunities we have in America. (These days, I continue to fight my 'immigrant mentality' because I always feel like I should be doing more and more and more — even when I've done enough.)

But that work ethic has proven very valuable to me. It pushed me to excel. If I came home with a B on my report card, I'd better have a darn good reason why I got such a low grade!

Mom especially put the pressure on her daughters to take advantage of our education. Mom was a very good student, but when she got pregnant at 16 by Viv's father, she was expelled from her Catholic school. So she had to get a job.

And four years later, she was impregnated by her boss — my 50+ year-old white male father, Otto Madsen. Theirs was not a love story — more like sexual harassment on the job. So my biological father was merely a sperm donor. Hence, I was born Carline Laroche — having my mother's maiden name and no ties whatsoever to my biological father.

The person who stepped into the role of father to me was Gerry. He legally adopted me later on and I became Carline Laroche Anglade. Gerry also wanted to adopt my sister Viv, but her father's family refused to give permission for the adoption. I remember feeling very sad because Viv's father's family actually wanted her — yet mine saw me as merely an inconvenience that should've been discarded.

Knowing that neither of my parents really wanted me gave me a drive to make a difference. To justify taking up space on the earth and to thank my mom for not getting rid of me.

… Like I said earlier, because Mom wasn't able to complete her education, she was determined we would. She didn't accept ANY excuses from us for not doing well in school. Actually, it was easy not to get in trouble at school, because I knew my mom would knock me upside my head if I did! I feared her far more than any peer pressure!

My childhood summers were mostly spent in Philadelphia. That's where my grandmother, Ruth Richard (a.k.a. "Mama Da") lived. Mama Da had seven children. The first three, Yolande (known as Yole), Maude and Yves were from her marriage to Dr. Vastey Parisien.

After her divorce, she had four more children: Michelle (my mom), Jacqueline (we called her Daty), Carole and Robert. This 'Fun Bunch' were from her … umm… 'Baby Daddy.'

My grandfather was a professional boxer named Jacques Laroche. He certainly was a ladies' man — my mom met several additional half-siblings much later in her adult life. It also turned out that one of my grandfather's relatives, Joseph Laroche, was the only black man on the Titanic when it sank on April 15, 1912. His Caucasian wife Juliette, who was pregnant with a son survived, along with their two young daughters, Simone and Louise. Joseph did not. But I digress...

Mama Da lived with my aunt Yole and her five daughters: Darnelle, Regina, Sandy (a.k.a. Moon), Pat and Shortie (her real name is Jude-Marie, but no one ever called her that!).

I didn't know we were poor. We always had food and clothes. And everyone else around me was in the same boat, so we were happy in our ignorance. During those summers, I got to spend a lot of time with Mama Da — and I saw that this woman knew how to make her way in the world.

Mama Da always said to me, "Pepette, you have to find a way to feed your family."

(And that nickname? It's pronounced "Pep-eht" — which imitates the sound of popped corn. It was given to me because I talked A LOT. No surprise there!)

Now, Mama Da was 50 years old when she emigrated from Haiti to the US. She didn't speak any English. She had no job. But that woman had hustle!

She could sew and she could spot an opportunity — and a market — a mile away. When she was in Haiti, she supported her seven children by setting up a business to sew uniforms for the guards and inmates at the local prison.

When she came to the US, she lost her business... but it didn't take her long to find a new income stream. We would go out to shop at the local market. Whenever she saw an obese woman, she would say to me, "Go ask that lady where she gets her clothes." I was seven or eight years old at that time. So I would go up to these ladies and say, "Excuse me, my grandmother wants to know where you get your clothes?" And I would hear over and over again, "Well, I have a hard time finding clothes. It's very difficult to find anything that's pretty or that fits me right."

Mama Da would always smile at the lady and say, "Tell her I can make her clothes."

And so began Mama Da's muumuu business! She saw a need and a desire that was unfulfilled. She simply gave the women what they wanted. Her prices were very reasonable and she had a large selection of fabrics that made her customers feel good about themselves. Her customers often stayed with her for decades. Later on, when I had a job, the best gift I could give Mama Da was bolts of fabrics. That way she could keep her overhead low and sell more muumuus!

I didn't realize what a powerful marketing lesson Mama Da was teaching me. When I write copy today — I say to myself, *"What does my prospect want — and how do I give it to him?"*

Mama Da discovered another side hustle that turned all her grandchildren into her 'employees.' She worked for a mail order company packaging blue and yellow plumber's tape. She was paid a per-piece amount for folding up the gooey tape. Then she would box them up and ship them back to the company to get paid. So every day during summer vacations, us grandkids spent a few hours folding those sticky blue and yellow strips. At the end of the week, Mama Da 'paid' us with money for the ice cream truck! Life was good! (I heard decades later from family members that the blue and yellow gooey tape is now used as the strip in Ziploc® bags!)

It wasn't long before I tested out my own entrepreneurial skills around the age of 9. We lived in Chillum Manor, a large apartment complex in D.C. and I needed to make some money. So along with my friend Dianne Turner and a few of the boys in the complex, I decided to knock on the apartment doors and offer to take the neighbors' trash to the dumpster. Then we'd go back to each apartment to collect our pay. This was my first experience in door-to-door sales — and it's where I quickly learned to target my market.

Some of those apartments had women with lots of kids — and LOTS of nasty, stinky trash! They would take us up on our offer — but only paid us a few cents. However — I found out there were other apartments with older, single males who thought it was so sweet that pretty little girls like me and Dianne were offering to help them. Even when they didn't have any trash, they would say, "Hold on honey! Let me find some-thing!" A few minutes later, they'd come to the door with a small bag containing a few crumpled pieces of paper. And then they'd give us a whole dollar for that little bit of trash!

They became our premier clients. Dianne and I let the other kids take care of the stinky trash and low-paying customers!

A few years later, at around age 11, my mom decided to sell Avon. But she was shy about knocking on doors and her English was still a little choppy. So I told her I would take the catalogs to her prospective customers and sell the products. She was fine with that. I brought in the sales and Mom fulfilled the orders. That was my first experience with joint ventures!

When I was in high school, I needed money to buy my pom-pom uniform. Mom said that wasn't a necessity — so I had to pay for it myself. I was about to take a job earning minimum wage, which was $2.30 per hour. But then I found out that the local shoe store, Thom McAn, was paying $1.50 per hour, but offering commission. I asked the manager to explain what 'commission' meant. And when I discovered I could control my paycheck based on my ability to sell and even upsell — I said, "Sign me up!"

Selling shoes was another great lesson in learning to identify my market. I quickly realized not to go after the tired mom with lots of kids, trying to pay as little as possible. No. Go after the dad whose wife forced him to go to the store! He just wants to get home so he can watch the game. So I would say, "Sir, you sit right there, I'll take care of everything for you as quickly as I can!"

Then, of course, I would come back with the shoes

for his little girl — AND a purse, stockings, socks, belt — just about all the accessories the kid could have (and which paid a much higher commission than shoes). Those dads appreciated the convenience and personal service I provided. And they were so eager to get out of the store, they would buy most of my recommendations!

Of course, I would take care of the customers who weren't my prime market... but I would hurry up and get them out of the way so I could focus on the big spenders — who, by the way, were oftentimes 50+ year-old white males.

So while my friends were making $2.30 per hour, I was making well over $5 per hour! I got the money for my pom-pom uniform much faster — thanks to those commission checks rolling in.

It was a priceless education... and a hint of things to come!

The Beginning Of The Rest Of My Life

Mickey Cole said the first time he ever saw me, I was getting off the school bus. It was the first day of North-western High School and we were both 15 years old. He said I was wearing a yellow top, white painter pants and Earth shoes. I don't remember seeing him, but his description of my attire that first day was correct. I remember meeting him in Mrs. Benson's tenth-grade English class. We were seated alphabetically, so thanks to my adopted last name starting with 'A' — I could casually look over to my left and see the students whose names started with 'C.' That's when I saw Mickey Cole seriously answering Mrs. Benson's question — with two pencils sticking out his nose! I busted out laughing.

I thought he was cute, exotic-looking (he's part Sioux-Indian) and goofy. He was smart but he tried to hide it. And he was hanging out with the wrong crowd — the kind of guys who would end up in jail, on drugs or dead. He kept a cigarette behind his ear — but I never saw him smoking. He wore this necklace with a Cancer zodiac sign. He tried to have an afro, but his hair was so soft that his 'fro' looked like a floppy black cloud! He cut class a lot and that was a big turn-off for me. But I did think he was cute.

The next school year, we had a history class together. And Mickey had really changed. He was showing up for class and paying attention. The cigarette behind the ear was gone. His hair was cut down much shorter and the Cancer necklace was gone. He had stopped hanging out with his crew and he was more focused.

He told me he was planning to get on the honor roll — and I laughed in his face! He had been goofing off so much I didn't think he could do it. But we were in the same study group and I could see he was serious. I wanted to know what had made this change in his life.

He told me he and his mom, Judy Thomas, were studying the Bible with Jehovah's Witnesses. It gave him direction, answers and the push he needed to make some changes. He had also realized he'd end up in jail if he kept going down the road he was on.

My family was Catholic, but I'd never heard about the things Mick was showing me in the Bible. The only Bible we had at home was bound in white leather and placed in a glass container on top of the china cabinet — completely out of reach. It was in pristine condition my entire childhood… because we never used it. I was baptized as an infant and had my formal confirmation at the age of 14 — but I had no idea what that really meant or even what we believed. We went to confession on Saturdays and Sundays; we'd show up 10 minutes late for the half-hour mass and leave five minutes early. That was the extent of my Catholic education.

But Mick was actually using the Bible and applying it to his life. He was showing me things I had never seen before. The first scripture he ever showed me was Matthew 23:9: "Moreover, do not call anyone your father on earth, for one is your Father, the heavenly one." Mick asked me what I called our priest and of course the answer was, "Father!" His next question seemed fair to me: "Why?" I didn't know the answer, so I made it a point to ask my favorite priest, Father Timothy Slevin at Nativity Catholic Church.

Father Slevin was a cool priest. He had long hair, played the guitar and wore a t-shirt with the slogan, "Go to Heaven with Father Slevin." I thought for sure he could give me the right answer! But when I showed him the scripture and asked him why we call him Father, he just smiled at me and said, "OK, you can call me Tim." What? My mother would've ripped my ear off if I called him Tim, but that was an "Aha!" moment for me.

This priest, who was supposedly a 'Man of God,' blew me off and offered no spiritual direction or education. And then there was this 16 year-old boy showing me things in the Bible that were life-changing. Father Slevin's nonchalance sparked a desire in me to learn more about what the Bible had to say.

(As it turned out, Father Slevin was *not* a cool priest. Decades later, I was shocked to see on TV that he had been arrested on pedophilia charges.)

My interest in the Bible continued and I began studying with Jehovah's Witnesses. I made lifelong friends during those early days of Bible studies — these people became part of my tribe and I continue to count on them for their friendship and advice down to this day.

At 17, Mick and I went out on our first 'date.' I say 'date' because even at that age, my mother didn't allow me to date! But when I told her it was just a bunch of kids going to the movies and getting something to eat afterwards, she said OK. In the Jehovah's Witness faith, dating is very serious. Its intent is to get to know someone with marriage in mind. So it's not just a casual activity for teenagers who are unprepared to marry. And although I wasn't raised as a Witness, my mother sure had that mentality! But her reason was much more focused: she did NOT want us to get pregnant!

At that time, I had also received a partial scholarship

to the school of my dreams, the University of Southern California (go Trojans!) to study broadcast journalism. By 18, I was a freshman, living in Los Angeles and pursuing what I thought was my dream.

I wanted to be a TV news anchor and I was thrilled when I got to do a phone interview with Connie Chung. A successful woman of color, I considered her a role model. But when she described her life and schedule, I started wondering if this was the right direction for me.

The dedication to being successful in the broadcasting field would have to take first place in my life. Did I want to really make the news world my main focus? Would that really bring me the happiness I wanted? Would my secular focus crowd out my spirituality? I didn't see how I would be able to pursue those goals and still have enough time to worship Jehovah and raise a family.

I realized that I was no longer willing to give my career that precious first slot.

When I had applied to schools, I had also been accepted by my second choice, The American University. I had enough credits that I would be able to graduate a semester early if I transferred, so I decided to move back home and go to AU. Graduating as soon as possible was really important to me: although I had received partial scholarships to these two private and very expensive schools, my loans had climbed well over $40,000… or equivalent to about $105,000 today!

And now that I had decided not to pursue broadcast journalism, I had no idea how I was going to repay those student loans. I decided I would just have to trust in God to find a way to make it work. My spirituality needed to hold that first place in my life.

I was baptized as one of Jehovah's Witnesses on June 27, 1982. Mick and I were now engaged and making plans to get married. My Mom asked us to please wait until after I graduated. She wanted me to get that diploma because she knew things could come up in marriage (like children!) that could derail my school goals. Boy, was she right! Mick respected and loved my mom — and we agreed we would wait.

I graduated from The American University on January 30, 1983. I only remember that exact day because it's when my favorite football team, the Washington Redskins, won Super Bowl XVII. The speakers at the graduation unanimously agreed to cut down the ceremony time so that all in attendance could get home in time for the big game. The graduation ceremony was forgettable — but the game was not.

My first job after college was selling radio ads for a local radio station called WINX. Their slogan was, "The station that has an affair with its community." I was the only female on the sales staff. The all-white male staff was fine with that slogan — but it sure made it difficult for clients to take me seriously!

I did learn to sharpen my sales skills while working at WINX. The sales team consisted of our sales manager, Gene Allum, an elderly, crotchety man named Irv Lichtenstein and me. Irv scared me. He was really mean. But I was determined to win over this 50+ year-old white male. I found out what he liked... the kind of music he enjoyed... and I listened to the numerous stories of all the aches and pains he experienced. I didn't realize then that Irv was preparing me for a career of writing to people just like him.

Anyway... I'd been putting off selecting a wedding date while working at WINX because I wanted to save up and travel to Europe again.

When I was 15, I had been invited to join the Foreign Student League. My mom worked a lot of extra hours to save up the money for me to go. We went to Europe for the month of August — it's the cheapest time to go because every country is practically closed for the summer — but hey, I didn't care. I was in Europe! I told my mom one day I would repay her and take her to Europe.

We got to visit London, Paris, Rome and Montreux, Switzerland. I have a really cool picture from the trip — it's a sketch of me made by a street artist in Paris. It's still one of my prized possessions. I've always felt that you grow when you travel. It takes you outside your safe little circle and makes you realize there are other cultures, other lives out there that are very different from yours, but that are amazing just the same.

My treasured Paris sketch, age 15

I travelled as much as I could afford to in my late teens — and when Mick and I got engaged, I told him we couldn't get married until he got a passport. We were going to go places!

I finally made the decision to pick a wedding date after a particularly frustrating day at WINX, dealing with yet another creepy client commenting about our radio station's provocative slogan. I just picked up the phone and told Mick, "OK — let's do this!"

It was August and we lived in Maryland. I told Mick I didn't want a winter wedding, so we picked October 8th — which was just six weeks away.

My sister had gotten married the previous year and Mom went all out for her wedding. So, when I called Mom and told her we'd set the date, she gulped. She said she only had $2,500 for my wedding. I said, "No problem — we will make it happen!"

We planned the wedding for 200 people. I got a beautiful dress on sale in a bridal store for $80 and we used my new 1983 Honda Civic as our limo. As a gift, my father-in-law, Melvin, took care of the food and found us a free place to hold the reception. That $2,500 budget even covered our honeymoon to the Poconos Mountains for three nights! It wasn't fancy — but it was the best wedding I've ever had!

When we came back from our honeymoon, I was dreading going back to work at the radio station. Mick said I should just quit and find something else.

So I did — and about six weeks later, I found out I was pregnant!

I had no insurance, barely any work experience and because no one wanted to hire a pregnant woman full-time, temp work was my only option. Man, we struggled! Mick was working as a welder and wasn't getting paid regularly. Some nights I laid awake wondering what had happened to the easy life I was living just a few months ago!

Fortunately, we had several friends who were in the same boat. So when the cabinets and refrigerator were bare, we would have a party! We would invite our friends over and pool our resources to create meals that would s-t-r-e-t-c-h. Ronnie and Maria's pack of chicken... Greg and Debbie's green beans... Helen and George's canned tomatoes... Derrick and Maxine's ground beef... Crystal's bag of rolls... Phyllis and Oscar's cookies... and voila! We would create an amazing meal together — and have leftovers to take home!

Ten and a half months after we were married, our daughter Milan Carlea Cole was born. Since we didn't have insurance, I tried to save money on the prenatal visits by going to a midwife. But by my ninth month, Milan was still breech. The midwives only delivered 'normal' babies, so I had to find an obstetrician in my last month of pregnancy. The midwives referred me to Dr. Rafiq Mian, who helped me with a vaginal footling breech delivery. Yep — Milan came out feet first!

That delivery cost us $20,000… on top of all those student loans. We were drowning in debt.

I still hadn't figured out how to do the wife thing yet — and now I was somebody's mother! But Milan was such a beautiful baby, I couldn't help but fall in love with her. Within a year, our finances started getting a little better, because Mick had joined the Prince George's County Fire Department. That gave us steady income — and we now had medical insurance.

So when our second daughter, Tiara Michelle Cole, came along, the medical bills from my pregnancy cost less than $200!

But by now, our neighborhood was going downhill. I freaked out when a 5 year-old child was accidentally shot in the crossfire of a drug deal gone bad. That could've been my child.

We needed to move… but we were in that weird financial bracket where we made too much money to be poor and too little to be middle-class.

Fortunately, my friend Lori Anderson told me about a program created to help middle-income people — teachers, nurses and firefighters — to buy homes in nearby Montgomery County. The local government was concerned that the county was too affluent and needed to be more diversified. I was sure glad about that! We qualified to participate in the "Moderately Priced Housing Program" by the skin of our teeth — we scraped in by just $500!

Even with interest rates over 11%, that program allowed us to purchase our first home: a new, 3-bedroom, 2-bath townhouse with an unfinished basement for $63,000 — which was $20,000 below market value in a nice neighborhood. So now, we had a mortgage, two kids and I really needed a job.

TWO

Stumbling Into Direct-Response
Copywriting

I had no idea what the direct-response market was about. I just needed a job.

My husband and I agreed that no matter what, one of us would be home with our kids. I was able to stay home while having the first two kids. Now, with my school loans demanding larger payments and the additional medical bills, money was tight!

By now, Milan was 2 ½, Tiara was 1 and I needed to find a part-time job that had a flexible schedule so I could work around Mick's firefighter shifts.

One day, I stumbled on an ad for a company that was 15 minutes from my house. It was a direct-response marketing company named Phillips Publishing. They were hiring customer service reps, paying $8 per hour. The money was not great, but what appealed to me the most was the next line in the ad: "Flexible schedule!"

I interviewed with Anne Marcelino, the customer

service manager. She was *so* enthusiastic when she spoke about the company. She loved working there and said it was a great entrepreneurial environment. I still had no clue what the industry was about but Anne said she could work with my need for flexibility — so I said yes to the job offer.

Well, Anne was right. It turned out to be an amazing environment. No matter who you were, your ideas and suggestions were welcomed.

The president, Tom Phillips, often walked the halls of the company saying, "Hi folks!" He knew my name before I even knew who he was. Tom treated his employees with respect and he valued our contributions. And he wasn't afraid to show it.

In 1993, Tom thanked us for our efforts and surprised the entire company — with an all-expenses paid trip to Disney World with our families. That was so remarkable that our company was spotlighted on the Today Show and in newspapers around the country!

Phillips takes staff and family to Disney, 1993

Phillips gave me a first-class education — far more valuable than the education that my student loans had paid for. And to this day, being a customer service rep was the best job I ever had to learn about the direct-response industry — that's where I learned to listen to my customers and give them what they need.

While I was learning about customer service, I was also looking for ways to grow in the company. One day, in the lunchroom, I spoke to an accountant named Jeannie Burcham, who told me they were looking for an Accounting Assistant. Jeannie and I got along great and she talked her boss, Carl Paladino, into giving me a shot — even though I had no accounting experience. The job paid $2 more per hour and I would be able to keep my flexible schedule. So, after six months in customer service, I transferred over to the accounting department. The pay increase helped… because during my two-year tenure in the accounting department, I gave birth to our third daughter: Jael India Cole.

I had no idea at the time that the transfer to the accounting department would turn out to be a very strategic move. Why? Because nothing happens in a company without going through accounting!

That's how I heard the company was planning to start up a brand new health division. Until then, Phillips was a financial publisher. Now they were broadening into a field that really interested me. I thought, *"Man, this is cool — I wanna get in on that!"*

Now, I had no experience whatsoever in marketing. Never took a marketing class in college. But this felt right. And the corporate culture was that talent could come from anywhere.

Still, trying to get an interview for this new division was not easy. Everyone was busy. Managers were trying to fill jobs with qualified candidates. And I had no experience. I couldn't blame them, but I knew I would have to take matters into my own hands.

The Sweatiest Three Hours Of My Life

I had an ace up my sleeve... and I used it to my advantage. Every Friday, I had to stay as late as necessary to compile the weekly results for the "Green Sheet." Tom called this report the Green Sheet because it represented the company's daily revenues. My job was to plug in the final numbers for the week and then hand-deliver the Green Sheet to the senior-level executives — including Bob King, the vice-president of the soon-to-launch health division.

Normally when I delivered the Green Sheet to Bob, he would be working on something at his desk. He would say, "Thank you, Carline"... but very seldom would he look up. Then I would leave to distribute the report to the other executives, so I could go home.

Well, that was not happening this time!

I walked into Bob's office, holding the Green Sheet. He saw me coming and greeted me politely, but as usual, he kept working, looking down, waiting for me to hand over the Green Sheet.

But I didn't.

Instead, I kept the Green Sheet just inches out of his reach. He had to look up. And when he did, he saw my smiling face, saying, "Nope! You can't have it until I get an interview for a job in the new health division!"

He just stared at me. I was scared to death. I thought he was gonna fire me on the spot!

Then he tilted his head like he was perplexed. Then he shrugged his shoulders and said, "OK." He pulled out his calendar and gave me a date and time. All I could think to say was "… Thank you!" I dropped the Green Sheet on his desk and hightailed it out of there before he changed his mind!

The interview was a week later, on a Friday afternoon. Thanks to Mama Da and my friend Maria Herrera-Brown, I had developed some pretty great sewing skills. I decided to wear one of my favorite suits — a Chanel-style suit I had made. It was a Kelly green jacket with navy blue trim, gold buttons and a fitted green pencil skirt. It was gorgeous.

But during that interview, I sweated right through it. Not only did I end up with huge sweat stains, but the fabric even crumpled up from all the moisture. By the end of the interview, the suit was ruined. I could never wear it again!

I've had many interviews since then — for much more senior-level positions. But that interview with Bob King, for an entry-level job as a marketing assistant, was the most intense interview I ever had in my entire career.

I was in there for almost three hours being grilled by the senior vice-president of the company.

He asked so many random questions and I didn't understand why he was asking many of them. He wanted to know where I shopped... what book I was reading at the time... what I would do on a free Sunday morning... what kind of sports I liked to play...

"Really?! These are the interview questions?"

I could not get my head around it and the questions just kept coming. I'm not saying they were all hard... but Bob didn't react to anything I said. He was like a blank page. I was on the spot and he wasn't giving me any indication about how the interview was going.

He was tough and at some point in the interview, I figured that I wasn't getting the job and I had nothing to lose. So I went on the attack. I stopped answering his questions and made him talk. I even told him some of my best jokes... and he still didn't crack a smile.

Finally, I got fed up. I asked him why he was asking all these random questions.

Bob simply said, "You're interviewing for a marketing job. Everything in your life has an element of marketing in it. If you're reading a book, I'll ask you what you're reading. If you're playing a sport, is it a team sport or individual? If you're shopping, I'd want to know what you're buying. Getting to know people is all part of marketing."

As it turned out, Bob King was one of the most brilliant marketers I've ever met and an amazing mentor to me. He could zone right in on what the market wanted.

He was not a social guy — definitely an introvert. But Bob knew you have to respect people no matter who they are... and not just for what they can do for you.

When Bob interviewed a candidate, he would do it with the same intensity whether it was for a part-time position to clean the offices at night, or for a senior-level management position. I was really impressed by that.

He gave everyone the respect they deserved and many years after my own interview, Bob told me, "I'm not hiring to fill a particular position. I'm hiring for the potential growth I see in the candidate."

Erica Beyer Bullard is probably one of the best examples of Bob's hiring strategy. Erica had just graduated from college when she interviewed for an editorial assistant position. Bob told me he wasn't interviewing her as an editorial assistant. He was interviewing the future group publisher of the division. Well, Erica went on to run Phillips Publishing (now known as Healthy Directions) as a senior vice-president.

Bob believed if you just hired someone for that immediate position — you were short-selling them and yourself.

(So unbeknownst to me — just about every question Bob asked me during my interview tied into something I ended up doing in the many different jobs I had in my career at Phillips.)

When I finally walked out of the interview, I was soaked in sweat and so bummed out. I just knew that I blew it. I even told Mick that I wasn't getting the job.

I moped around the whole weekend and didn't

want to go to work on Tuesday. But then on Monday morning, I got a call from the group publisher of the new division, Marshall Hamilton. He said, "Good morning Carline — welcome to our team!"

I was so surprised that I asked if he was sure he had the right person! I told him that my interview did not go very well. Marshall said, "Well, according to Bob, I need to get you on our team immediately."

Not only was I hired, but Bob gave me an instant raise. Instead of the marketing assistant position, Bob promoted me to assistant marketing manager.

And just like that — I became a direct-response marketer!

My early colleagues at Phillips gave me some incredible on-the-job experience. I knew nothing, but I was a fast learner and these folks were sharp and willing to share their knowledge.

Lorna Newman was a wonderful mentor who always told it like it was. Wendy Marsh saved the company hundreds of thousands of dollars using her negotiating skills with printers and mailers. Annette Payne knew how to segment lists to generate the most revenue from rented names.

Sue Tomasso, John Baldwin, Prescott Bullard and Dave Ferry turned the list-rental business into a phenomenal profit center.

Julie Noble and Kim Krause Schwalm helped launch a very lucrative vitamin business. Marji Ross and David Franke were editorial geniuses. Richard Stanton-Jones was a creative powerhouse who wasn't afraid to take risks.

And the administrative support team (Phyllis Merrill, Mary Nebel, Rebecca Johnson Stanton-Jones, Christina Hill and our beloved front-desk beauty, Millie Cousins) kept everything moving and grooving.

I sucked up whatever knowledge I could get from these folks — and so many more — to help grow our new Health Group.

For the first year, we struggled like crazy. The Health Group started off with one newsletter: Dr. Jorge Rios' *Cardiac Alert*. It was a small break-even product and there was no way we could exist with this newsletter alone. We needed a whole lot more!

We tried several attempts to launch traditional health letters, such as the *Scripps Clinic Health Letter* and later the *George Washington University Health Letter*... both bombed.

Things were starting to get desperate. And then...

... One day, our editor David Franke introduced us to Dr. Julian Whitaker. This guy was a maverick! He had attitude. He wasn't afraid to take on the medical establishment. He was a natural leader and he had a vision. Dr. Whitaker wanted America to know about natural treatments that worked as well — or even better — than prescription drugs and their nasty side effects!

We had a champion — and now we needed to give him a voice.

There was no doubt in Bob and Marshall's minds about who would be the copywriter for Dr. Whitaker's

Health & Healing newsletter. A-level copywriter Clayton Makepeace was already delivering successful financial copy for the company and he would be the one to give Dr. Whitaker a voice for our market.

At this time, I was pregnant with my fourth child. So the team was always joking about whether Carline the Marketer or Carline the Mom would deliver first!

Clayton met with Dr. Whitaker to get to know and understand his vision. After that meeting, Clayton spent a weekend in a hotel room and wrote the entire package. His promotion was ready to test.

On June 1, 1991, I gave birth to my son, Chadam Thomas Cole. A month later, on July 1, 1991, we launched the first issue of *Health & Healing*. Mommy won.

While I was on maternity leave, Marshall would call me practically every day to give me results. The launch mailing of Clayton's *Give Me 90 Days* promo was a blockbuster success! We were getting 4% and even 5% response rates — and sometimes even higher — on the mailings. Those numbers were INCREDIBLE in this industry and still are. We had hit an untapped nerve and the market responded wildly! I even worked during my maternity leave to create more mail plans to send as many pieces of Clayton's control as possible.

I don't think anyone had any idea how successful *Health & Healing* would be — except for Dr. Whitaker. When we first met him, I remember seeing his passion. He spoke like a wild man. He knew America needed his leadership. You can't fake that! Dr. Whitaker even told

Tom Phillips that he would bet him $100 that this would be the most successful product Phillips ever had. Tom graciously declined that bet, saying we were all in this together.

With the birth of *Health & Healing*, our little Health Group — consisting of group publisher, Marshall Hamilton, editorial manager, David Franke and now newly-promoted senior marketing manager, yours truly — was no longer the black sheep of the company. We were getting respect and attention… and we needed help.

When I returned from maternity leave, Wendy Marsh had transferred to our team as the new marketing director. Wendy's job was to grow *Health & Healing* as quickly and profitably as possible. It was during this time that we both got to meet the creative, brilliant copywriter who had launched *Health & Healing*.

After Clayton's package did so well, he decided to visit Phillips. It became a company-wide event. Wendy and I were working in the back office, selecting names for the next mail plan. We eventually came out and joined the party.

I was kinda nervous to meet Clayton, so that's when I cracked my infamous joke: "With a name like Clayton Makepeace, I envisioned a tall Native American guy with a feather on your head — not a blond, blue-eyed teddy bear." And the room went completely silent. Thank goodness Clayton busted out laughing! All the tension in the room melted away and we became instant friends.

I had no idea Clayton would change the course of my career!

Carving My Own Path

Back in the 1980s, the direct-response industry was a predominantly white male world. My bosses were white men. My vendors were mostly white men. Yes, there were a few women in management positions — but we were few and far between.

As we were growing *Health & Healing*, I needed to find new list brokers who could help us find new lists and new markets. I came across a small list company named Country Marketing. I called and spoke to the owner — a woman named Susan Nabinger. We hit it off immediately. Susan could find very different lists that *worked*. Because she ran a small company, she knew she couldn't compete with the big list brokers — so she focused on finding unique sources for new names. She came through for me in spades!

Susan became a force to reckon with in the industry. She's a feisty Jewish New Yorker who's used to having to fight for everything. I just loved her 'take no prisoners' mentality! She was also the mom of two sons. So it was refreshing to see a woman who had successfully 'been there and done that' in a male-dominated industry.

One particular experience will always give Susan a special place in my heart. I had to attend a business trip in New York. The day before I left, two of my kids were sick with bad colds. I felt bad about leaving but I also knew a cold wasn't life-threatening. And they were in good hands with their dad. I was in a dinner meeting around the time the kids would be going to bed and I was feeling down that I couldn't talk to them. We were nowhere near being done for the night, but Susan quietly pulled me out of the meeting.

She opened up her purse and pulled out a cell phone. It was a monstrosity compared to today's iPhone! I mean, that thing took up most of her purse! She handed me that brick of a phone and said, "I know you probably want to call your kids and say goodnight to them. Go ahead — I'll cover for you. Come back when you're done."

It was so thoughtful and while it might sound like a small gesture, it was a powerful act of friendship to me. I found a quiet corner to call my kids and say goodnight to them. And then I could focus on my job again.

Besides Susan, I didn't know too many other women who had successfully raised a family in this industry. Phillips was a young company. Many of the women were either single or married with no children. And I certainly didn't know of any women of color who were married and had kids.

Being a mom was tough in that environment… and trying to breastfeed was a nightmare! I remember coming back from maternity leave to find out that our offices had been replaced with open cubicles. The first thing I thought was, *"Where am I going to pump?!"* There was no breastfeeding lounge and the bathrooms didn't even have a corner where you could place a chair and sit. The men making those decisions just didn't think about it.

When I was promoted to director of marketing, I had to focus even harder to keep my priorities straight. At times it was disheartening to hear a female colleague make a disparaging comment about my family life. I remember sitting in a board meeting one Wednesday night and the meeting was dragging on unnecessarily.

By 7pm, I'd had enough. I finally stood up and said I had to leave. One of the other women in the room rolled her eyes and said, "Oh, she probably has to go home to her kids again."

I wanted to smack her head off! But I kept it together, forced myself to smile and said, "Yes, I do! Goodnight."

Many years later, one of the women in that boardroom apologized for making it difficult for me. She said, "It wasn't until I had kids of my own that I realized how thoughtless those words were. The stand you had to take at that time must have been so difficult."

And yes, it was difficult. But I had to accept that I didn't have a path to follow and that I would just have to carve out my own.

I was beginning to believe that you can have everything you want… just not at the same time. Mick and I were working together to make sure we accomplished our main priorities — and not let the other stuff drag us down.

But it was getting tougher. I actually left Phillips and

took a job at Georgetown Publishing House as executive vice-president in Washington, D.C. working with a man named Dani Levinas and a wonderful woman named Lois Willingham. I learned a lot working on the business-to-business side of direct-response marketing. But ultimately, after two years at Georgetown Publishing House, Phillips wooed me back. But my job was now in the investment side of the business.

Bob wanted me to help one of the struggling products. It was a newsletter called *Ken and Daria Dolan's Straight Talk on Your Money*. I was also in charge of the company's largest circulation financial newsletter, *The Retirement Letter*. Plus, Bob wanted me to find new business opportunities for the company, including setting up cruise seminars. During this stage of my career, I got to work with some really great guys including Tobin Smith, Chris Marrett, Howie Present and Tommy Thompson — just to name a few.

I stayed at Phillips another two years, but my life was feeling out of balance. My boss wanted me in the office more and my husband and kids wanted me home more. I was feeling pulled like a rag doll and something had to change. I started looking for other options.

By this time, I was working closely with copy. But once I knew I wanted to make a change, I started focusing on the copywriters themselves. These guys — who were mostly 50+ year-old white males — were living all around the world... working on their own schedule... and raking in big bucks. I thought to myself,

"What's wrong with this picture? Why can't I do what they're doing? I've got to at least try, right?"

So after 12 years at Phillips Publishing, I sat down with Mick one night and said, "I'm ready to quit my job to try copywriting."

THREE

Hanging Out My Shingle

B ob King fired me from Phillips Publishing in
October of 1998.

My plan to quit my job had been coming
together slowly. Mick and I talked and prayed about it
and finally I was comfortable enough to make the
move.

My strict 'Debt Eradication Program' enabled us to
get rid of all our credit card bills and a car note. I
didn't know what kind of income to expect in my first
year as a freelancer. I was about to give up a six-figure
income and I thought if we could live on half of that
income, we would be OK. In fact, we would be more
than OK — because I would now be in control of my
time!

During this transition planning, I called Clayton for
advice. He had critiqued several of my in-house writing
projects in the past few years and I trusted his opinion.
So after I told him about my plan, he said, "I would

never try to talk you into leaving my Number One client... however, WHEN you do leave, call me."

Man — that was just the boost of confidence I needed!

A few days later, I had a meeting with Bob King to turn in my letter of resignation. Bob refused to accept the letter. After I explained my frustrations about my current situation and the new goals I had set, Bob just looked at me very sternly.

He said, "If you quit now, you're free to walk out. I won't stop you. But if I fire you, based on your tenure in the company, you can walk away with six months of severance pay."

"Well, please fire me, Bob!"

He said he would... on one condition. I had to stay until I finished my current project. I was spearheading the company's first investment cruise seminar. Bob said we had 700 of our best customers attending that Caribbean cruise — and he wanted everything to go right. If I followed through on this project and it came off victorious — then he would fire me.

He would also let me stay until the end of the year and use those last few weeks to get myself set up in my new business. With this six-month severance agreement, Phillips would, in essence, become my first 'client'!

I just LOVED that man!

My momma didn't raise no dummy — so I agreed immediately. The cruise seminar was a phenomenal success and when I came back to work, Bob fired me! I was incredibly grateful for his support and guidance throughout my years at Phillips.

Bob always said that as marketers, our mission was "to make people better off in ways that they desire... and will pay for." I'm glad I got to tell him how much I respected him as a marketer and a person before he passed away on March 16, 2018. His generous offer allowed me to work on my freelance business — without the stress of having to bring in income right away.

So, on January 1, 1999, I hung out my shingle as a copywriter and launched Cole Marketing $olutions, Inc. and I called Clayton that same day!

Right away, he told me he had a client he wanted me to meet: Martin Weiss, Owner of Weiss Research. Clayton was handling Martin's copy, but they needed help in the marketing department with mailing list selections. Now, selecting lists wasn't what I really wanted to do. I was now a freelance copywriter! But the money was good and I needed clients. I knew if I did a great job for Martin, it would give me some clout in the industry.

So I agreed to help create mail plans — targeting 50+ year-old white males — and boom — I was creating income for my business!

That project lasted for seven months — and it gave me the opportunity and confidence to go after other clients. It was also around this time that Dave Nelson from Walter Karl List Brokers called me. He was looking for a black male copywriter for his potency clients.

I talked my way into that job (see the introduction if you missed that story) — and got my first control. Now I had a story to share with prospective clients. Until this point, I was cold-calling the marketing directors and owners of companies I wanted to work with, letting them know I was available to write copy.

The first thing they always said was to mail them samples of my controls for review. I didn't have any controls yet, so they quickly dismissed me. But with my new male potency package, I could now say…

"I Know You're Busy — So Let Me Send You My *Most Recent* Control!"

So what if I only had ONE control? It was recent!

It's all about how you position yourself. When I was a marketing director, I would get swamped with samples from copywriters. I never read their copy from cover to cover. I usually glanced them over and picked one to read — I was too busy to read everything! So I used that knowledge. I let my prospective clients know that I understood how busy they were — and that I was going to make their lives much easier by just sending my "most recent" control for review. Wasn't that so thoughtful of me?

And it worked! People started returning my phone calls and I was getting on the shortlist for future projects. A few marketing directors did ask to see more of my controls — but I just said, "Sure, I'll send them to you later, but let's talk about how we can work together first."

Once I got a second control, I changed my pitch slightly to send "my two most recent controls"... as opposed to my *only* two controls! See? It's HOW you say it that matters!

You've got to remember that when you're a free-lance copywriter — your first client is YOU!

You've got to spend time and learn how to market yourself. How to come off confident, but not arrogant. You've got to learn to be persuasive. And you've got to believe in yourself!

My business was starting to take off. At the end of each year, I created a sales letter called *Carline's Kick-Butt Year.* I put in photos of the controls I had written and told a little story about each one: what the product was, the industry it was in, how it was positioned for the market and so on. And I ended the page by saying, "Let Me Write the Next Kick-Butt Control for YOU."

I intentionally mailed the sales piece (yes, in the actual mail — I didn't have email yet!) to competitors of the products I had written controls for. Why? I knew the competitors had probably received these packages in their mailboxes. Now I wanted them to know who wrote that copy — so they could hire me to do a great job for them too.

And it worked!

I started getting phone calls from large players in the health market. My name was getting out — and they were willing to give me a shot! And every time I got a new package to work on, I would find something Clayton had written previously — and then reverse-engineer it to create my package!

If he had an anger-driven headline, I'd find a way to get angry too. If he had a skeptical lead — I was going to say "Hogwash!" just like him! If he offered five special gifts, then so would I! If he told the prospect that they reached a crossroad and it's time to act, I would lay out a very similar closing argument. Clayton was my template. And I just kept following that formula until I felt comfortable enough to deviate and create my own style.

I often asked Clayton if he would critique my packages — and he generously did whenever he could. My best comment from him was, "For a moment there — I thought I had written this. Love this and love you!" Can't get a better compliment than that from your mentor!

About a year after I worked on mailing lists for Weiss, Martin decided to launch a health newsletter and he wanted Clayton to write the promo. Clayton was swamped but he agreed — on the condition that Martin would bring me in to help. So, Martin, Clayton and I met with the Weiss team in Palm Beach Gardens, Florida, to brainstorm package themes.

The doctor who would be the spokesman for the newsletter was Dr. James F. Balch, a urologist and bestselling co-author of *Prescriptions for Nutritional Healing*. Having a prestigious urologist as our spokesman, we all agreed we should launch with a sex package.

Martin thought having a male and female copywriter working on this project would be ideal. So Clayton and I created the *Forbidden Secrets of Sex and Healing* promo.

The launch was a block-buster success! We all met again a few months later in Florida and Martin was brag-ging about the package in a meeting. And he was taking credit for putting this

Clayton and I wrote this promo together. It was a huge success and one of the best experiences in my career.

male/female copywriting team together. He compli-mented me for bringing in the sweet, delicate, feminine copy. And then he thanked Clayton for his rock-hard, sheet-ripping copy.

Clayton and I looked at each other... and we both busted out laughing!

Clayton told Martin he had it all wrong! He said, "That head-banging, heavy panting, put-the-lead-back-in-your-pencil copy was all Carline." And then I chimed in: "Yeah, Clayton wrote that gooey, lovey-dovey, girly stuff!"

The entire room broke out in laughter. This was one of my fondest memories of Clayton. He loved this story and shared it with anyone who would listen.

Nearly 20 years later, *Forbidden Secrets of Sex and*

Healing is still one of my most famous packages. It was my first blockbuster control and it mailed for several years. It was also the first time I saw how much your income can grow from royalties! We put a very large pool in our backyard with a royalty check from that package!

Carline's Kick-Butt Calendar

After the success of the *Forbidden Secrets* package — word got out. My schedule really started filling up. Clayton and I worked on another package for the Dr. Balch franchise — and got another control with *Nature's Amazing Brain-Savers.*

My second blockbuster control

Clayton booked three or four of my package slots well in advance. He didn't know what he would use them for — but he wanted me available when he needed me. And that was fine with me! I loved working with him. I learned so much and became a stronger writer with every package he copy chiefed!

I turned the *Carline's Kick-Butt Year* sales promo into an annual event. I created an elite client list and sent them an invite in August to book projects for the following year.

Why August?

Honestly, I don't know why that particular month worked so well. But I was trying to position myself as a sought-after copywriter. If I was contacting clients in November or December saying I was opening my schedule for January — that made me seem too available. Clients needed to book early so they could get on my schedule. And I needed to know what my income would look like for the next year!

Here's what I'd say in the email:

> "Hey [name of client], I'm putting together my creative schedule for next year. Since I've enjoyed working with you so much — I wanted to give you the first shot at choosing the slots that work best for you. I'm going to open up my schedule to others soon, so let me know if you want in — and how many packages you want to book."

I wasn't pushing for a sale — just giving the clients the opportunity to beat the rush and book now. The first time I sent out the invite, three of my slots filled almost immediately. The next year, five were snatched up. Today, I still open my calendar for clients to book projects in August. But I only send the invite to two or three clients — and I usually book my entire year in a day or two.

In 2015, I accidentally sent the invitation to someone who wasn't one of my 'elite' clients. We had talked about possibly working together — but I didn't make any commitments. His name was very similar to one of my elite clients and I accidentally included him in the email!

Before I even realized my mistake — he had emailed me back saying he wanted six slots! I didn't want to tell him that I had messed up — so I honored the agreement and we had a phenomenally successful year.

I worked with him on numerous successful projects for two years. When August came around in the third year, I sent the email out. But this time, he sent a message saying, "I'll get back to you in a few days." Well, I had a German client who was chomping at the bit to get on my schedule. When I told him I had an opening — he said, "We are interested in four to six slots." Then two other clients wanted three slots each. So by the time my "I'll get back to you" client got back to me, I had nothing available.

Boy was he mad!

It was awkward, but I was glad it happened. It let him know that even though I liked working with him, he wasn't my only client. I like working with all my clients. And the ones who take my schedule seriously are the ones who stay on my schedule.

Even though he was upset, I wasn't backing down. I told him I'd put him on my waitlist — after all, sometimes things change and it's nice to have a back-up if a client has to cancel a project. In his case, I didn't have any cancellations — so he had to wait another year before we could work together.

Now, my little 'elite list mailing' doesn't always work perfectly. One time, I sent out the email… and instead of booking eight to ten projects in a day — I only booked two projects in a week!

I decided I could look at it two ways. I could either panic... or I could look forward to a potential ten-month vacation!

I chose the ten months of vacation.

It was actually very freeing not to have my schedule completely booked. I knew something would come up — but I had no idea what. Turns out, AWAI contacted me to put together an online writing program. They gave me carte blanche to do whatever I liked. And that was the birth of a course called, *"How to Write Kick-Butt Copy Carline Anglade-Cole's Crazy Way."* I spent two months working on the program and that was time I wouldn't have had if my schedule was pre-booked. That was an amazing project — I'm very proud that it's helped so many folks find their voice and take the plunge into copywriting.

And by the way, I did eventually fill the other slots. I've learned not to sweat it anymore. Something will come up if you're open to seeing each moment as an opportunity.

"I'm Not A Doctor — I Just Play One In Direct Mail."

When I first started off, I worked with just about anyone who would give me a shot at writing copy. I loved writing and I knew I could be good at it. I just needed experience... writing samples... and a track record! So I took whatever jobs came my way. A client would ask if I could write about gardening — YES, I can! Investments? You bet! Renewal letters? Oh yeah! Special reports and premiums? Absolutely!

And then I had to figure out HOW to write what I promised to deliver!

So those first few years, I was a 'Jane-of-all-trades.' I didn't particularly like investment writing. The field was boring to me. I couldn't understand those stupid charts. And I just didn't feel like I was really helping the customer. The client, yes — but not the customer. I didn't like tapping into the greed factor in that industry. I wasn't loving the gardening, biz-op or self-improvement markets either. Those jobs were just a means to an end. I needed money. The client needed copy. And that was the end of the relationship.

But when I got a chance to write about alternative health — man, I came alive. I loved researching and learning about new discoveries and nutrients that were making a real difference in my prospect's life.

I loved talking with cutting-edge doctors who were discovering remedies and cures. I loved taking their 'doctor-ese' and turning it into a conversation my 50+ year-old white male market could relate to. And I loved that what I was learning at work was also helping my family, my friends and myself to live healthier lives! I've always been health conscious — but now I was working with clients who were paying me to read and study more about health. I found my passion! I had become "Dr. Copywriter!"

I often joked to my friends, "I'm not a doctor — I

just play one in direct mail." I knew the health field was the right space for me. So now, I needed to let health clients know they should hire me.

So I 'niched' myself. Ouch — sounds painful, right?

And it was at first. Every day I had to tell myself, "*I'm an alternative health direct-response copywriter targeting the 50+ year-old white male market.*" That was my work mantra. And then I had to turn down writing jobs that took me out of that niche. So, if an investment client called me up for a project, I would say, "No thanks — I'm focusing exclusively on alternative health, but I can refer you to another writer who can help you out if you like?"

By giving away jobs that weren't in my niche, I started getting more health projects!

The law of reciprocity is a powerful thing. In direct-response, we use it all the time. That's why we give 'free gifts' just for trying the product. It's an innate feeling that if someone gives you a gift, you want to find a way to reciprocate. That's just a natural part of human existence. It works phenomenally well in direct-response marketing. And I didn't realize it was also working with the referrals. Turns out...

... When I referred non-health jobs to other copy-writers, they started sending health referrals my way. It was a win-win. And it was great because clients were coming to me saying that I was highly recommended by a fellow copywriter.

OK — let me digress for a moment here. I say all this about 'niching' myself in the health market. But I did have one exception. I called it my "Oprah Clause." And it was simple: if Oprah ever called and asked me to write for her — I would abandon health copywriting in a heartbeat!

My "Oprah Clause" paid off!

Turns out, in 2008, I did get a chance to write a package for Oprah, designed by the amazing Lori Haller.

Julie Doll, the Marketing Director at Oxmoor House called me up one day and told me they had won the project to launch *O Magazine* via direct mail. She said, "Carline, I think you'd be great for this…" and I just about passed out! When I called up Lori to ask if she wanted to be my designer — she screamed so loud I nearly lost my hearing! This was a big break for both of us.

But it was a HARD job. We learned quickly that when you're working for a celebrity, there are many additional requirements. They had a team of people making sure we stayed "on-brand." But even though we had to jump through a lot of hoops, we LOVED it!

I got to answer Oprah's call — and I didn't have to abandon health copywriting after all.

OK — back to the original story. By niching, I now

had enough wiggle room to be more selective about my projects.

I decided I would turn down any project that didn't bring serious and positive benefits to my customer. I was not gonna help grow a crappy product. If I was not comfortable with the product — why should I try to sell it to my market? These folks are counting on me to look out for them!

I really believe that's been a big reason for my success. It's much easier to write strong sales copy and get controls when your products actually help people!

I look at it like this: I'm taking on a project that will consume at least a month of my life. And I'm at a stage in my life where I have less time going forward than I do looking backward. So I'm not wasting my precious time on a project I'm not going to enjoy. Now — don't get me wrong. I may still struggle and pull my hair out working on the project. But fundamentally, it's a project I can be proud to offer to my 50+ year-old white male market.

These days, I can keep my schedule full and only work with two or three clients a year. And that's because about ten years ago, I discovered that the more clients I had, the less income I made.

What?! Counter-intuitive, right?

Well, not really. As I reviewed my copywriting schedule through the years, I realized I had to shift gears whenever I wrote for a new client. Each client has his own nuances. His own legal department. And his own comfort level with taking risks. I had to make my copy conform to each company's policy.

And that takes a lot of time when you're working with a different company every month!

But when I worked with one company for several months at a time, there was virtually no learning curve. I understood their idiosyncrasies. I knew how they wanted to speak to their portion of the marketplace. So it was easy to get into the right mindset and start writing the copy.

I gave the clients who booked multiple projects with me top priority — it didn't matter if I wrote their packages back-to-back or spread them out through the year. I knew them and their business very well, so I could just pick up the next project and run with it.

So I started writing more packages for fewer clients and getting more successes!

For example, my 2019 schedule looked like this:

- Two promos for Client 1 in January and February
- One promo for Client 2 in March
- Back to Client 1 for three promos for April, May and June (with two weeks off for a Turks and Caicos vacation!)
- Two promos for Client 3 in July and August
- Back to Client 1 in September
- A month off for travel in October
- Back to Client 2 in November

- Finish off with Client 3 for two promos in November and December

Like I said, this schedule allows me to write more promos and gives me flexibility to include lengthy vacations, volunteer work and even 'goof-off' time. I like knowing who I'm dealing with and which projects we're going to be working on in advance. And it streamlines my work life so I'm not spending ridiculous amounts of time in client meetings or dealing with office politics. I hate that stuff!

On this schedule, Client 1 was my only new client. It was fun getting to know these folks and understanding their business model. Clients 2 and 3 were my 'bread and butter' clients. I've worked with them for many years. I know their products and how they want to talk to their segment of the 50+ year-old white male market.

And the majority of my projects are new launches. I LOVE launches! Why?

Because all I have to do is give the client a solid package that works in the mail and it's an instant control! I've got no competition. I don't have to beat an existing control. So, I have lots of freedom to really GO for it!

When my assignment is to beat a current control — I'm much more strategic. I try to find out what the current control is lacking and I attack its weaknesses! My job is not to deliver the best copy I can write — it's to BEAT the control! So sometimes that means I hold back on a little of my craziness. Once I've beaten the control — then I can unleash my creative madness. I have to remember that riskier ideas may not work... so I make more calculated creative decisions.

And I have to keep my ego in check.

If a client says they have a strong control they want me to beat, I'll pass on the assignment. Why? Because I'm not going to let my ego tell me I can beat that strong control. It's a strong control for a reason! It's WORK-ING! I want the fatiguing controls. The ones who've had their heyday and need to be retired. I want to bring new blood to the market. I want to beat the down-and-out boxer — not Muhammad Ali in his prime!

And I'm not the only one who feels that way.

When I was a marketing manager at Phillips, I found out that two of the best copywriters in the world had a 'gentlemen's agreement' not to compete against each other.

Clayton once told me that he and the legendary copywriter Gary Bencivenga decided not to go up against each other's copy. If Gary had the control, Clayton wouldn't work on the product until that control was on its last leg. And vice-versa.

They both knew that a Clayton Makepeace control or a Gary Bencivenga control was a CONTROL because they were doing a lot of things right! Sure, the promos could be beaten — but you'd have to be a heck of a writer to beat them while the promo was in its prime.

I certainly wasn't that good of a writer. And I didn't need to be. I like it when the odds are in my favor. Competing against a strong Makepeace or Bencivenga promo gave me a 20% chance, MAYBE, of success. There are lots of poorly performing controls that I have a 70% or 80% chance of clobbering.

Like I said before… my momma didn't raise no dummy.

FOUR

The Power of Story

O ne of the first purchases I made for my new freelance business was a black, three-inch binder.

It was to store my future writing samples. I really believed that if I could fill that one binder with my samples — not necessarily my controls — then I would be a successful writer. I had that vision locked in my brain.

As I write this book, I'm on binder #36 (and they're five-inches — not three!)

The majority of those samples are controls. And they contain stories. Successful weight loss stories. Death-defying stories. Discovery stories. Last-wish stories. Accidental breakthrough stories. These stories appear in the headline... on the cover... in the lead... in side-bars... in the close... and anywhere else I can fit them in!

That's because stories are powerful.

Whenever I needed a story and felt stuck, I used to call up Mama Da and tell her we were going to Walmart. Remember how she used me as a kid to get her muumuu clients? Well, it was payback time! She was an absolute people-magnet — at 99 years old, people thought she was in her late 70s. Folks trusted her instantly, so they would tell her all kinds of things — right there in the aisles at Walmart. I would just stand close by... listen... and sometimes prod Mama Da to get more juicy details!

That's why it's very dangerous to be my friend.

I tell people all the time that if they become my friend, I'm probably going to find a way to put one of their stories in my sales promos — and I might not even change their names!

This is one of the most important things I can teach anybody about copywriting: tap into the power of story. If you're not telling a story in your sales copy — find a good one and write about it.

Too Much Information? No Such Thing!

If I know somebody's got an issue with their health, I have no problems asking, "Are you willing to share your story?" If the answer is no, then I'll butt out real quick. But if you're my friend — you know I'm going to want to hear all the gory details.

My friends know they're not allowed to have anything gross happen to them without telling me about it in vivid detail. Some of them look forward to seeing how long it will take for me to turn green!

Now, I'm really not trying to be nosey. For one thing, I am interested in their health. And I'm curious. But I also want to know how they handled the situation… because they may be able to help thousands — if not millions — of other folks in the same situation.

For example, my friend Shannon was telling me about her dad's diabetes. He wasn't taking care of himself and he developed neuropathy. She said his foot looked horrible. It was swollen, tight and forming all kinds of pus and cysts. She apologized for grossing me out, until I asked her to take a picture of his foot! She said, "Ewww, Carline — are you serious?!"

Absolutely!

She sent me a picture of her dad's foot… and I immediately emailed her back and said, "That foot is so disgusting — I'll pay you a hundred bucks for the picture!"

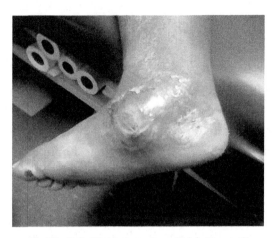

The "Dad's foot" picture gave me a kick-butt control!

That photo — which I called "Dad's foot" — became the cover of a blood sugar package I wrote a few months later — and it was a control for three years! People could simply relate to Shannon's Dad. They could see that his situation could easily happen to them. And they REALLY didn't want to end up with a foot that looked like that!

I have no shame. I will use anything and everything.

One time I was working on a hemorrhoid project. I sent out an email to my friends saying, "I am paying real good money if you're willing to share photos of your hemorrhoids! I promise I will not show your face and I will change your name!"

And people did it! Those photos went in that sales promo — and it kicked butt (pun intended)! When readers saw that they weren't alone with this problem, they wanted to know how others got relief. Maybe there was hope for them too!

Stories are everywhere. You just have to be willing to ask questions, to dig deeper into the story... even when it's awkward or uncomfortable.

Remember — if you don't ask, you don't get!

And once you've asked... shut up and listen! Sometimes that story will evolve right before your eyes. For example....

... A while ago, I was working on a digestion package with my daughter Tiara. Her first draft was weak — and I just couldn't figure out how to give it that UMPH! Then a friend came to visit for a weekend. She was a missionary living in Liberia... and she had been having stomach problems for years.

Doctors thought she had parasites, so they put her on an extensive parasite protocol. But even after all the treatments, her stomach was constantly gurgling. She could barely eat... but she was gaining weight. The cramping hurt like crazy. She couldn't figure out what was going on.

And then she told me that she hadn't pooped in three months!

What the heck?

At this point, I told Tiara to start recording because I KNEW there was a big idea for our package somewhere in this story. Then I asked my friend...

"How are you even still alive?"

She jokingly said she thought the whole thing was a blessing because she was living in a developing country with very poor sanitation — so not 'going' was a good thing. But then she gave me even more vivid details.

When she ate, the food would get "stuck." She would be miserable for hours. She became a vegetarian to help her symptoms, but even cooked vegetables posed a problem. She had been on antibiotics for six months. She didn't know anything about probiotics, so she was feeling miserable and catching every illness going around. She went through months of medical testing.

Doctors thought she had gastro-esophageal reflux disease (GERD)... then they gave her enemas to force her to poop. But nothing was happening. She had to go to the emergency room for the doctor to physically manipulate her bowels until she was finally able to "go" after three months.

I couldn't make this stuff up! Her story was exactly what we needed for the digestion package.

Another story came from visiting my friend with dementia who lives in a nursing home. She had been there for almost a year. I knew her family and congregation members had been visiting regularly. When I got there, she recognized me immediately and we had a great conversation. We were catching up on old times and then she suddenly said, "You know, I just got here last week. You're my first visitor." I thought, *"Wow... she seemed fine, but I know that's not true. Her memory really IS going."*

Do you see a story there? I got the idea for a memory loss promotion immediately:

> *"When you're having a conversation with an old friend over coffee, do you worry that something's wrong? Do you feel like you might be repeating yourself, or like maybe you've said something that's not quite right? Can you remember if you showered this morning, or the last time you saw your kids?"*

When you find a personal story like that, something that has real emotion in it, you can always find a way to work that feeling into your copy. Stories like these are everywhere. Finding them is just about being in tune with your surroundings.

Of course, you won't always have a perfect story fall into your lap for every package. When I was in my early thirties, I created focus groups to help me to get to know my market. I didn't understand menopause — so when I was working on that project, I asked my friends in that age group to come over for dinner and talk to me. I'd ask, "When you're having a hot flash, what happens? What does it feel like? How long does it last?" Then I would listen to their "personal summer" stories.

I created similar focus groups for arthritis, memory loss, impotence — just about every project I worked on. Now, fast forward 21 years and I AM my market! I don't need other people to tell me what joint pain, low blood sugar, or brain farts feel like. I'm living with it every day!

But no matter what the package is, or whether I'm

familiar with the market or not, my goal when writing any piece of copy is to find the story.

If a client offers me a choice of projects to work on, I pick the project with the best story! I believe we are fundamentally hardwired for stories. When you put a child down to sleep, what does he want to hear? A bedtime story! When you hear, "Once upon a time…" — what are you about to get? A story!

When I can tap into the power of a story — I know I've got a great chance of getting a winner. And frankly…

… Without a story, you're just listing a bunch of facts. You're talking at the reader — and not connecting with him. And stories allow you a tremendous amount of flexibility. You can start at the end and then work back to the beginning. You can start in the middle and create a cliffhanger. And your story can have a happy ending, or a sad one.

Your Own Stories Are Powerful!

Americans usually want a happy story. Europeans tend to tolerate — and even expect — a sad ending. Me? I love 'em both! Oftentimes I try to set up expectations. If it's going to be an unhappy ending, I'll say, "Let me warn you now… this does not end well."

I don't want my reader to get so sad that he doesn't buy the product, obviously, but I want to find a way to make the story so strong that he feels like he has to act now!

I recently experienced my own sad story. And as part of my healing process, I incorporated my story into a project.

I had agreed to write a package for a client with a beet juice formula that improves circulation. It was a great product, but they were struggling to find the right message that resonated with the market. They wanted to give it one last shot — and they flat out told me if my package didn't work, they were going to discontinue the product.

We met in December 2018 and agreed we should try a very positive direction, talking about how the nitric oxide in beet juice opens up your arteries for better blood flow so you can enjoy life to the full again.

Then a month later, in January, 2019, my stepfather Gerry got very sick.

He had to go to the hospital because he was having problems with his leg. He didn't take good care of himself and the doctor told him he had very poor circulation in his left leg. It was so bad that the doctors said he needed surgery to try to restore his circulation.

If the surgery was unsuccessful, they would need to amputate his leg.

Gerry told them, "You can do whatever you need to get the circulation flowing, but you can't amputate my leg." The doctors performed the surgery but it wasn't successful. To make matters worse — they discovered that Gerry's right leg also had poor circulation. They recommended that both legs be amputated if he was going to survive.

Gerry said, "If I wasn't going to let you cut off one leg — I'm definitely not letting you cut off two!"

Fourteen days later, Gerry died.

After the funeral, I flew back home and it was time to get back to work. I was supposed to write this happy, upbeat package about healthy circulation — but all I could think about was how poor circulation had just killed the man who raised me.

I wasn't feeling happy. And I definitely wasn't writing happy. I just decided to write a cautionary tale, using Gerry's story — the only detail I changed was switching his name from Gerry to Jerry. I talked about how he ignored the pins and needles and cold hands and feet — both early signs of poor circulation. Then I talked about how the symptoms got progressively worse until he finally had to act. But it was too late. I took the reader to the operating room... to the family conversations... to the 'what-ifs'... and to the regrets.

I told the reader that Gerry's story wasn't unique at all. It happens all the time but I don't want it to happen to him. After I told the whole story, I transitioned into the product:

> "Now — please know this: I'm not saying [product] would've saved Jerry's life. That would be very presumptuous of me. But I am saying this...
>
> ...if you're experiencing signs of poor circulation now — [product] may save YOU

from a health disaster — if you take action
while there's still time!"

Man, I was in the zone when I wrote the story. I was processing my own grief and disbelief that something like numb heels and dead skin on your feet could be early warning signs of something so severe…

… But there was just one problem.

I kinda forgot to tell the client that I had completely changed direction on this package.

When I sent them the final copy, I got an email saying, "Uh, Carline, this isn't what we talked about and agreed on…"

Oops.

I told them, "My bad — I'm just not feeling chipper right now." This is the message that spoke to me and that's what I wrote. I told them to trust me on this. I asked one of my favorite designers, Rob Davis, to work with me on this project.

And here's how it turned out:

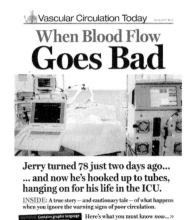

My family's story became a sad warning about the dangers of poor circulation.

The cover reads:

"When Blood Flow Goes Bad:

Jerry turned 78 just two days ago... and now he's hooked up to tubes, hanging on for his life in the ICU.

Inside: a true story — and cautionary tale — of what happens when you ignore the warning signs of poor circulation."

My client is very thankful he listened to me because the copy kicked butt! It's still a control. And the product that was almost discontinued — is now one of their best products! It's now helping thousands of folks experience healthy circulation again!

Jerry's story was so compelling that it also worked

for a completely different product — about calcium plaque — for the German market. I just switched Jerry's name to Peter!

So if you're ever looking for a good story — look at your own life. Realize that you're not unique. If you're experiencing specific health problems, your market is too — especially if you're a 50+ year-old white male.

FIVE

Learn The Rules — and BREAK 'Em
Whenever You Can!

There are a lot of 'rules' in copywriting. And I say you can break just about any of them!

Sure, these rules are important and exist for a reason — but once you know WHY, you can defy 'em — and have some real fun with your copy!

Today you can find a lot of copywriting programs — and many of them are very good. But they can be very systematic and regimented. I think if I started out trying to master a '20-Step Program to Writing Great Copy' — I probably would've flunked out... or at least been bored out of my mind.

I blame my Myers–Briggs ENFP personality type for that!

To me, trying to follow a structure kills my creativity. And it's not fun. I like to have fun when I learn and work! I've always learned the best — and had the most successes — when I experimented and challenged the status quo. And it was fun breaking those rules while getting paid to do it!

On-the-job training taught me to be very instinctive with my writing. If I learned a 'copywriting rule,' I wouldn't dismiss it. I just didn't make it *my* rule. I'd keep it in the back of my mind — and then I'd try to find a way to break the rule and forge another path.

When I first started working as a copywriter, one of the main rules I was instructed to follow was the 'seven-words-or-less' headline.

I was told, "You get more success with short headlines. It's been tested and proven for decades." Many clients insisted on short headlines… they wouldn't even let me *test* longer headlines! That just never made sense to me. It's not the number of words — it's the impact of the words that will get a prospect to buy.

But I was a rookie with no track record, so I had to pay my dues… at least for a while.

Another annoying 'rule' — and this one REALLY drove me nuts — was that a copywriter had to deliver the headline and a lead before actually getting the paid assignment.

And even worse — the client wanted an OUTLINE! I absolutely hate outlines. I was the kid in high school who wrote the term paper first and then turned in the outline to the teacher afterwards. My brain just does not work in outline order.

To this day, I very seldom know where I'm going when I start to write a sales promo. I just go with the flow and let the story and research take me on a journey. So I became very frustrated being forced into a regimented copywriting structure.

So when I was starting out, I would make up fake outlines to placate clients. But I never followed them. My copy always ended up completely different! It frustrated the clients — they thought I was being difficult — but I was just trying to give them what they wanted... even though it's not how I operated.

Depending on the project, I may want to start working on the order form first. Or the testimonials. Or the sidebars. The idea for my lead may come from those elements in the package. And most often, the headline is the LAST thing I write. This process made sense for my wacky brain. But it didn't work well with the company's marketing folks who wanted to micromanage their copywriters.

These were big-name clients in the health industry who were willing to give new writers a shot — but it had to be on their terms. I get it — they were taking a risk on a new writer, so they wanted to control the process to avoid as many losses as possible. So they gave the writer their writing protocol and expected to be kept in the loop during the entire writing process.

But that was suffocating me... so I either fired those clients, or was fired by them.

I needed to find clients who would let me write copy and then let the market decide if it had value. So I started saying no to delivering headlines before I wrote the copy. I said no to submitting multiple leads. I ignored bogus deadlines to monitor my progress. I took a stand and said, "You're hiring me to write you a control. Leave me alone and let me do my job." That did not go well with the large clients — but it resonated very well with the smaller mailers who didn't have time or the manpower to oversee copywriters — and these folks became my favorite clients.

I found that small to mid-size companies didn't care how I wrote the copy. They didn't even want to know my 'writing process.' They didn't have the time to micromanage me. They wanted winners. Oftentimes I was working directly with the owner of the company. He (and 90% of the time it was a 'he') had to trust me to do my job. And I loved the freedom to be as creative as possible.

The Only Rule That Matters

The only rule I make a point to stick to — and seem to follow instinctively — is the rule of being true. Be true to what you're doing and to yourself. This is about having integrity in yourself and your work. So before I take on a project, I ask myself...

- Is it really a good product?
- Is it going to help people?
- Is there proof that it works?
- Have other people used it and gotten the results they expected?
- Would I let my mom, husband or friend take this product?

I have no desire to help bring a worthless product to the market and take advantage of unsuspecting folks. But if I know the product is credible and it can deliver a real benefit to the customer, then all I have to do is tell a great story. And that story can come from the client, the product, from satisfied customers — just about anywhere.

This is easy to do when you work with ethical people who have good products to sell. But you still have to do your part as the writer.

And it's up to you to make the product a star!

It's up to you to find a unique way to connect that product with your prospect. To show your customer why he really needs this product, right now. To engage your reader and convince him to trust you enough to shell out his hard-earned moolah. If you can do that — then you're on your way to creating a winning promotion.

But the rule of being true also applies to being true to yourself. If I'm not excited about the product... if I don't feel I can really bring something interesting and of value to the customer... if I'm just not 'feeling it' — I'll take a pass and let the client know it's not the project for me. I'll encourage the client to find another writer — or recommend someone — who will be more excited about working on the project than I am. I know myself. I won't do a good job if I'm not excited or interested in what I'm doing. And I don't want to waste a month of my life being bored!

My rule of being true applies to clients too. I'm very

big on vibes, so I'll pass on working with a prospective client if he rubs me the wrong way. I may not be able to put my finger on it — but if something feels weird, I'm out. There are a lot of sleazy, fly-by-night companies in this industry. And I've been able to avoid many of them because of my highly tuned 'take flight' instinct! For example...

... About 15 years ago, a mailer (let's call him 'John'), contacted me to write a promo for a joint pain formula. Within a few minutes of our phone conversation, I thought, *"Man, this guy is arrogant!"* But arrogance alone doesn't mean I won't work with someone. The deal-breaker occurred when we talked about his guarantee.

Now, I believe every mailer should offer a guarantee. That tells me the client believes in his product and it protects the consumer. And most of the time, it's just stupid marketing not to offer a guarantee of some sort! Well, John said he wasn't offering a guarantee because his customers "would try to screw him over by using the product and then returning it to get a refund."

That comment said a boatload about John as a person and a businessman. Even if that statement was accurate — I bet it would apply to less than 5% of his mailing list. But what bothered me the most was what he thought about his customers. It was so negative! He wasn't looking out for their interest. He wasn't trying to develop a relationship that would last several years. He just wanted to make a quick buck and didn't give a squat about the people who put their trust in him and his product. So I didn't want to help him grow his business one bit! At the end of the conversation, I told him I wasn't the right copywriter for him and wished him the best.

Now, I know it might seem crazy to turn work down just because you don't really like someone — especially when you're a struggling young writer. But if you have a bad gut feeling, or you know you don't function well in certain situations — listen to that vibe. It will probably save you a lot of headaches down the road. Don't set yourself up for failure!

Yeah, you might be able to get the work done. But you won't be happy — so you might as well have stayed at the 9-to-5 job you hated before you became a freelance copywriter.

The biggest benefit of the rule of being true is that when I finish my packages, I love them! I think the product will help people. I feel I'm making a positive impact on the health market. And I'm proud of my work. When I can sit on my hands and read my copy — and think, *"Man, I need to buy this stuff!"* — then I know I've done my best work and I'm ready to send the copy to the client.

And my clients know when I send them the copy — it's final. Yes, it needs to be reviewed by the legal department for compliance. Yes, the client can make suggestions and comments. But we're not doing line edits. It's not a draft. Most likely, the copy won't get much better than this.

By the time the client receives my copy — it's

already gone through dozens of drafts and edits. After legal changes — the copy is ready to be tested, as is! It's not going through a committee that wants to suggest tweaks and new ideas. Not at this point. It's time to test and see if I hit a nerve with the market!

And if I don't hit that nerve, I own my mistakes.

I want every package I write to become a control. So if the client tests my package and it doesn't work — I'm going to take that copy and rework it until I can beat the existing control. I don't charge the client for these changes and I will give him five or even ten new cover tests. We'll try a new lead, a new offer… I'll dissect that package to figure out what went wrong. And then I'll do my best to fix it.

But that's only if it's MY copy.

If the client took my copy and butchered it with changes from the 'marketing committee' and it flopped — well, that wasn't MY copy! I tell him, "My copy is on the cutting room floor somewhere. I'm not interested in fixing what you sent because it's not my copy."

Fortunately, that very seldom happens these days. My clients know I take ownership of my work. But even so, the reality is that you can write great copy and sometimes the market just won't care. You can do everything right and it might still bomb. That's a hard pill to swallow but it's a truth in the direct-response industry.

Nonetheless — as a copywriter, you've gotta fight for your vision and you've got to stand behind your work. If it bombs — try to fix it the best you can!

So If You Ignore The Rules... How Do You Get Good?

The same way doctors, lawyers, engineers and teachers become successful! You study and work your craft!

Focus on writing strong, results-driven copy and you will rise to the top based on your successes. My goal was never to be an 'in-demand', A-list copywriter. I just wanted to write copy that was good enough to pay the bills and give me freedom to create my own work schedule.

That's an achievable goal for most folks, so focus on honing your skills. Study the masters. Treat their controls like textbooks. Heck — write out every word in their controls by hand if that helps you!

So how do you find out if a particular package is a control? Or who wrote it?

Well, if you receive the same package in the mail several times — you can safely bet that it's a control. A mailer is going to send his winning promotion to the majority of his mailing list. Yes, he will test other creative ideas — but if you keep seeing one particular promo in the mail over and over again — that's the control, so study that piece.

If you're going to be in the direct-response business — you need to collect samples of good copy. The best way to do this is to buy a product from a company you are interested in writing for. Let's say it's for the mailer called Peak Pure & Natural.

Go to their website, www.peaknatural.com, buy a product and get your name on their mailing list.

Now, you've become a valuable buyer and the company will start mailing you promotions for their other products. They'll also rent your name to other similar companies — and you'll start receiving promotions for those products too.

If you want to see how direct marketing companies cross-sell your name, alter your name slightly when you order that first product. For example, instead of Carline Cole, I may order as 'Char Cole.' That will tell me which companies Peak Pure & Natural rents my name to. And it's a great way to find out about new mailers that may become new clients.

As far as who wrote the promotion — well, that's a little trickier. Remember, as a direct-response copywriter, you're essentially a ghostwriter. You are the voice of your health guru. Your name won't appear in the promotion. However…

… Like I said earlier, I like to have fun when I write my copy. So, sometimes, I may try out the product and include my own testimonial. So if you ever see my name in a promo — it's most likely my package!

But in the end, it really doesn't matter who wrote the promo. If you've seen a package multiple times in the mail, study it even if you can't figure out who wrote it. That copy is working. Good copy is good copy!

That's what's so awesome about this industry. You don't have to be a famous copywriter. You just have to have a good idea that delivers great results to your client. Keep doing that over and over again — and you can become a kick-butt copywriter too!

Looking back, ignoring the rules was actually a superpower for me. I didn't get intimidated by all the marketing experts. I didn't get flustered with 'formulas for success.' I just studied the heck out of sales copy written by great copywriters like Clayton Makepeace, Gary Bencivenga, Don Hauptman, Richard Armstrong, Dan Kennedy, Kent Komae, David Deutsch, Don Mahoney, Bob Bly, John Forde, Gary Halbert, Parris Lampropoulos and Mark Ford — and then I put my butt into gear!

Yes — you have to know how to write compelling copy. But you also have to find YOUR voice and YOUR style. You've gotta trust your instincts and trust yourself enough to take calculated risks.

I've attended many copywriting seminars where the speakers encouraged writers to find the 'voice' or 'style' of their guru to make their copy stand out. I laugh at this now because I realized that in the past 21 years of writing copy, I wasn't focusing on the guru's voice at all. If I tried to talk like most of the doctors who represented my products — my prospect would be bored as heck! Those guys speak 'doctor-ese' and my 50+ year-old white male prospect is not going to relate to that!

So while I do spend time getting to know my guru and trying to pick up on his unique approach and nuances — I'm not writing in his voice. I'm actually giving the doctor MY voice. My easy way of talking to a customer. My ability to make a complicated idea simple enough for the prospect to say, "Aha!" So when I developed my own style of writing — I just shared that style with my gurus. Oh man — as I write this, I realize it might come off arrogant and that's not my intention. It's just the truth when I say that no matter what promo I'm writing, the prospect is buying my style of writing — and not necessarily the doctor guru's voice.

Here's the proof:

I've worked on several projects where we started off with one doctor guru. A few years later, for whatever reason, we needed to change the doctor. Did that mean we had to start all over and create a new promo with this new doc's voice? Hardly! Most of the time, all I needed to do was a 'search and replace.' I took out the old doctor's name, bio and personal info and swapped it with the new doctor's info. Headline stayed the same. Lead stayed the same. Copy stayed the same. And the package continued to work! So was it really the doc's 'voice' — or the killer copy?

Boom! Drop the mic!

Here's more proof. This one is a little more subjective, but still supports my claim. A few years ago, my friend Anissa came over to read some copy. Out of nowhere she said, "Oh my goodness — I heard you in my brain, Carline! I know the information is coming from that doctor, but I heard your voice talking to me." Then she said, "You write like you talk."

And that's ultimately the goal. As a copywriter, I know that I'm just having a conversation with my prospect. I'm telling that 50+ year-old white male what he needs to do now to feel better. I'm walking him through the process to explain why he needs this product right now. I'm showing him proof that the product works. I'm guiding his hands to pick up the telephone and ACT NOW — so he can claim his free gifts and get this amazing product at the lowest, introductory price available. And I'm protecting him with a 100% Money Back Guarantee. I'm being his friend. And he's going to reward our friendship by making that purchase.

SIX

The 'Carline Routine'

W hen we lived in the suburbs of Germantown, Maryland... I'm pretty sure our neighbors thought we were drug dealers.

They saw me going to the mailbox and regularly taking out checks. As a firefighter, Mick only worked two or three days a week and I was home in sweats and a t-shirt every day. I received frequent deliveries from FedEx and UPS. And we lived in a large house with a swimming pool and nice cars in the driveway.

A few neighbors actually asked me, "What *do* you do for a living?" I didn't make things better by replying, "I help people feel better in ways they're willing to pay for."

As the only black family in that exclusive 50+ year-old white male community... we stuck out like a sore thumb.

I think my daily routine also got their attention. But

it's a routine that has helped me experience a lot of creative success.

Now, I'm not saying you can't be a good writer without a routine like mine. But to be a prolific writer — you've got to be in the habit of writing regularly. And you've got to figure out where your writing 'sweet spot' is.

Are you a morning person?

Do you thrive in the afternoon?

Or do you come alive at night?

Me? I'm a super early bird. The earlier the better! I'm up and working by 5am — sometimes as early as 4am. I don't toss and turn at night. If I can't sleep — then I just assume it's time for me to wake up and I start my day.

One of the first things I do every morning is read an encouraging scriptural thought from my copy of *Examining the Scriptures Daily* — the *Daily Text* for short. I think about the positive message for the day and how I can apply it in my life. It gets me centered and reminds me to keep whatever comes my way in perspective.

Then, when I walk down to the kitchen, I paraphrase a thought from the *Daily Text* and write it on our dry erase board. It becomes my reminder for the day. The message might say something like, "Choose your words wisely" … "You're not hospitable if you only hang out with your homies"… "Jesus died for me. Make that sacrifice count"… "Don't seek the Kingdom Second"… or "The REAL life is yet to come." The message on the board just needs to speak to me — and hopefully encourage my family as they see it throughout the day too.

If I'm working with an international client, I may start working while still in bed. The client is usually six or more hours ahead of me, so I've got several emails waiting for me to answer. I'll often spend 15 to 30 minutes responding to their pressing questions.

Then I brush my teeth, throw on some workout clothes and head to the kitchen to make my green drink. Some of my clients have green powders, alkalizing drinks, beet juices or superfoods that give you the nutrients you need for the day. I mix up my concoction of powders in a 20-ounce shaker cup, toss in a swig of apple cider vinegar — and start guzzling it down. That way I just have one yucky drink a day!

I take my vitamins along with the swigs of the green drink. Now, the vitamin pills I take vary depending on the project I'm working on for the month. I am the kind of writer who believes in taking the product I'm trying to get my customers to buy. So, if I'm working on a cardio promo, I'll take the client's cardio formula. However, I do draw the line when it comes to taking male potency products! Hey — I may write as a 50+ year-old white male — but I'm still a girl!

Then, I head down to my basement office. I've tried working in other rooms in the house, but having a designated space far away from my family makes a big difference in my productivity. I use the hour or so before sunrise to review yesterday's copy and think about what I want to do today. I'm just putting fodder in my brain.

When the sun comes up, I'm ready to work out. I run five to six miles every other day and on the opposite days, I do weight training and then enjoy some time in the sauna. I don't love to exercise — I just love the results I get from exercising. I feel like the air is going in one ear as I'm running, taking the gunk and cobwebs out the other ear! It just gets my mind and body working together.

But I also have a secret weapon I use during my running time. I call it the "Sandy Factor."

Sandy is my cousin, Sandra Ferguson — who I call "Moon." It's a French childhood name derived from "Mamoune" — which means "my little person." As we got older, I just shortened and Americanized it to "Moon." She only allows a handful of family members to call her Moon. So if you ever meet her in person – don't you dare call her Moon! Everyone else has to call her Sandy. That's why I have to call it the "Sandy Factor" here, instead of what it really is — my "Moon Factor"!

Sandy is my sounding board. When I'm working out — especially when I'm running — I'm often on the phone with her tossing ideas, headlines, leads... anything is fair game. She'll tell me if she loves or hates the idea — and why. That's proven extremely valuable to me through the years. And it actually got her an 'accidental career.'

Sandy is great at finding deals online. And she does

amazing work researching products before she makes a purchase. So, one day, I was working with Layne Lowery at Health Resources on a new launch. We needed someone to research ingredients for us. I told him I had just the right person.

Layne hired Sandy as his company's researcher. She was scared to death of the job but it paid $35 an hour, which was great money for her at the time. I told Sandy she was already doing research for friends and family — this was just a more focused research on health products. Then I told her, "Fake it til you make it!" And she did.

She got me great stuff to use in my promos. Then she picked up a few more clients along the way and eventually, Ferguson Research Group was launched! A few years later, I was interviewed by AWAI and told them how I get my great research. They loved the story I shared about Sandy, so they contacted her and made her the guru for their very successful Internet Research Program!

But back to my morning routine. Imagine me running — and running my mouth — as I go around my neighborhood for six laps. All the neighbors see is what appears to be a crazy woman talking to herself and running around in circles.

Maybe they figure I must be taking those drugs I'm selling!

Anyway, by the time I've finished my hourly run and talking to Sandy nearly non-stop — the endorphins are starting to kick in. My brain feels sharp... my energy level is high… and I'm excited to get to the computer!

I take a shower and I'm usually at my desk by 8:30am, ready to write. The hours between 8:30am and 1pm are my 'Money Time.' I get more writing done in that window than any other time during the day. So it's important for me to guard that time — cuz mama gotta pay the bills!

When my kids were still little, I had to make some adjustments in this schedule so I could get them off to school. But now that everybody's grown — I fiercely protect my 'sweet spot' writing time.

By 1pm, my creativity doesn't decline — it TANKS! I'm not kidding. I don't feel like I have a creative bone left in my body. So I don't fight it. I just make sure to plan my afternoons with meetings or other non-creative activities. By 2pm or 3pm, my day is done. But before I stop working…

… I do one simple trick: I leave the writing project in mid-thought.

In other words, I leave my writing with a cliffhanger. I'll leave a note to myself that says, "Finish this idea tomorrow". Or "Tomorrow — need a killer sidebar about X". My brain doesn't like incomplete thoughts. It wants closure. So this forces my subconscious mind to keep searching for a great closure-creating idea while I'm off doing other things!

This little trick also prevents me from wasting time the next morning trying to find a place to start. My subconscious has been thinking about a solution for me all night long. And many times — an idea pops up as soon as I'm ready to start! Love when that happens!

Carving Out The Angel

When I start working on a sales package, I know that somewhere in the mounds of research and tons of testimonials — a great idea is hiding. I just have to figure out what that idea is. And that reminds me of the famous quote from Michelangelo:

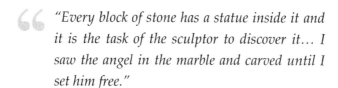

"Every block of stone has a statue inside it and it is the task of the sculptor to discover it… I saw the angel in the marble and carved until I set him free."

Sometimes you don't know what you've got until you start chiseling.

And that's why I hate outlines! Like I told you in Chapter Five, my clients used to request an outline, or a lead and headlines before I started the package. I can't be confined like that. I just want to chisel away until the angel appears!

But there's one thing that always happens to me as I stare at that solid block of marble — I develop a bad case of 'Imposter Syndrome!'

The symptoms are very severe.

You'd think I'd be immune by now, but I still catch it often. Every time I start a new promotion, I think, *"WHY did I say yes to this project? I have no idea what I'm doing! My life was FINE and now everyone's gonna finally realize I don't know anything. I'm a fake! I suck, I suck, I suck..."*

When that happens — and I'm not kidding you, it happens with just about every promo I write — I take the antidote.

I just start reading.

I say to myself, *"OK, you don't know squat about this product. So take the time to learn. Don't write anything. Just be the consumer."*

In his book, *On Writing*, Steven King says:

> "Writing isn't about making money, getting famous, getting dates, getting laid, or making friends. In the end, it's about enriching the lives of those who will read your work and enriching your own life, as well. It's about getting up, getting well and getting over. Getting happy, okay? Getting happy."

So when I get a case of Imposter Syndrome — I remind myself that all I'm doing is writing to my 50+ year-old white male market and telling him about something I think would help make him healthier. I try to make that info interesting, fun and easy to read.

I also want to give my market a 'face.' If my client tells me their research skews to a 70+ year-old market, I'll Google popular names from the 1950s and choose one. So I'll make my 'hero' a Thomas or Mary and then

I'll add James, Patricia, John, Michael and Susan as potential supporting cast members as I develop the promo.

I pick these common names because there is a high probability that the person reading the promo will see his or her name, or the name of someone he knows well. And that might help us to bond. I started using popular names for the core market years ago when I heard Harvey B. Mackay, author of *Swim with the Sharks without Being Eaten Alive*, give a speech at a marketing seminar. Harvey said the most powerful word in the English language is a person's name and that you should use it often.

(By the way, the letter "J" is one of the most popular letters. When I worked at Georgetown Publishing House, we created post it note mailings that were signed by "J." We tested other initials — and "J" always clobbered them all!)

When Your Writing Feels Stuck, Do This...

I love this quote from Gene Fowler:

> "Writing is easy: All you do is sit staring at a blank sheet of paper until drops of blood form on your forehead."

Staring at that blank page at the start of a project is killer. Even when the project is brand new and I haven't done a single minute of work on it, I do everything within my power NOT to start with a blank page. You can do this too, even if you don't have a clue what you're going to write about. Even if your creative juices just aren't flowing. Even if you think you suck as a writer — you don't ever have to stare at a blank page again.

Here's what you do…

Just open a previous project you've worked on. Then, copy the key elements you're going to need for your new project — and paste it on the blank pages of the new document!

For example…

… You know you're going to need a headline, so on the first page of the blank document, just write, 'BIG FREAKING HEADLINE GOES HERE' in Impact 36 type font. Wow — you've got a headline. Yes, it will need some tweaking, but it's a start!

Now, you know you're going to need a bio from your guru. So if you don't have it yet, just grab any other guru's bio and drop it in the package. Now you've got a bio sidebar!

You're going to need testimonials — so if you've got some, just start reading through them. Get to know what people are saying about this product. Copy the good testimonials into your document. Don't edit anything, just cut and paste. Do the same for the order form, the guarantee and any other static piece of copy you're going to need for your promo.

I promise you — by the time you finish this exercise — you're going to have 10 or more pages of copy —

and you haven't really written anything yet! You've just overcome the blank page blues!

Then take a break. You've worked hard.

Tomorrow you can go back to chiseling that marble and finding a piece of that angel.

I also read a lot at this stage. If I'm selling a health book, I'll just keep reading through the chapters until I stumble on an "Aha!" moment. I've already got my Word document open on my computer — so I just jot down whatever I find interesting in the book. Maybe it's something cool I've never heard of before. Maybe it's a way to save time. Maybe it's a surprising discovery. It doesn't matter — I just jot it down. I don't worry about fixing typos or editing at this stage. I'm just chiseling away at the marble.

Eventually a theme begins to appear.

It can take days before I find the right approach, but in the meantime, I've found so many facts and juicy stories that I can create great sidebars... pull quotes... and even cover tests I know I'm going to need!

When I really don't feel like working — or when I want to goof off — I give myself a deadline with a reward. I'll say something like, "*OK — research for 30 minutes then stop. Read testimonials for 30 minutes then stop. After two hours of working — you can take off the rest of the day.*"

If stuff isn't flowing by that two-hour deadline — then I end my writing day.

It's just going to be painful staring at the screen otherwise. So I get out of the office and do something fun. And while it may look like I'm goofing off for the day — my brain is still working. All the research is in my brain. I'm just allowing it time to process.

Then I come back the next day and I may start my writing day just asking this question: *"What would I tell my mom about this product?"*

So, I'll write, "Dear Michelle…" and then start talking to my mom:

> *"You know what Mom? You're getting up in the middle of the night feeling panicky. You're tired, you feel like your brain is mush, you keep saying, "the doctor says I'm fine!"… but you know you're not fine. You don't want to worry your children but what if something is wrong? Really wrong. Now you're feeling even more afraid. You know you can't ignore the warning signs, especially when you're experiencing… [need 6-8 bullets here]"*

Yeah — I know it's choppy copy — but I don't care. I'm just talking to my mom. I can edit later. Right now I just need to get a conversation going. If I think it would be great to have a quote or a scientific study while I'm writing, I don't mess up my flow by going off to find the info. I just make a note that says, "Need a quote here" or "Put a study here" and I just keep it moving!

I can get a researcher to find specific info for me later. Let me tell you a true story about what happened to me the last time I tried to research info at this early stage of the writing process:

I was getting stuck working on an arthritis project. So I thought, *"Hmmm, maybe I should research different types of arthritis."* As I'm Googling — I see gout. *"Hmm...gout — that's arthritis of the foot. Hmm... foot — I need some shoes."*

Next thing you know, I'm ordering six pairs of shoes online!

I only bought the shoes because it was less painful spending the money than going back to work! But I wasted half my 'Money Time' for that day. Lesson learned — don't get distracted!

How To Write Promos FAST

The reason I'm able to write successful promotions is because I *just write*. I don't worry about getting all the research together first. Sometimes I write the package and I have no concrete information whatsoever — no studies, nothing! But I've got a cool story and I just focus on that.

As I'm writing the story, I'll make a note whenever I need to support the statement. Then I keep writing until I feel like I've really told the story.

The best promotions I've ever written were just conversations between the writer and the prospect. Two buds chatting it up. I didn't care about the copywriting 'rules'. I just wanted to talk to my buddy in a fun and relatable way:

> *"Listen, the doctor says it regenerates this cell type and stimulates that protein — but forget all that stuff. Let me tell you something.*
>
> *You're going to be shocked when you wash your face in the morning.*
>
> *You'll be wondering where your wrinkles went!*
>
> *You know, this treatment has been around for 2,000 years. Egyptian queens used to have people paste it all over them. They had to sit there for hours and be frozen like mummies — but when they got out — wow!*
>
> *Their skin looked as smooth as the day they were born!"*

Writing great copy is just writing a letter to a friend, sharing your enthusiasm, your belief and the confidence that what you're saying will help the person reading.

When I write like this — when I'm excited and love the product and want to tell somebody this story — my job is sooooooo easy!

Once I've got that creative story right — then I've got a solid first draft! By keeping it light and not worrying about getting all my research perfect up front, I can write faster copy.

When I've finished my first draft — then it's time for my analytical side to come out and say, *"Alright Ma'am — you've made these outlandish claims — now PROVE 'em!"*

I know copywriters who take months to write a package while they try to get every little detail perfect. MONTHS! I would die of boredom!

You don't have to get everything right in your copy. Flaws are OK. Perfection is not expected.

In fact, trying to perfect your copy is a big mistake! Keeping the writing casual and friendly makes it come off sincere. It's not prefabricated, so it makes the reader feel like he really knows you and that you're looking out for him.

If I'm talking to a girlfriend, I'm going to use some words that aren't quite perfect English. I'm going to start sentences by saying 'but'. Halfway through a sentence, I may change direction, then come back to the original idea later!

Think about it. When you're talking to your buddy or your spouse, you're not worried about getting all your grammar completely correct. You're not worried about making linear arguments. That's just not how people talk when they know each other!

I like to put my own spin on the Leonardo da Vinci quote, "Art is never finished, only abandoned" — and make it one of my favorite reminders: "Copy is never finished — it's only abandoned!"

So if you're trying to make your copy perfect down to the very last detail — STOP! You're really just procrastinating. You're probably afraid to turn in the copy because the client may not like it. You're afraid of rejection. STOP!

There will always be something you could add or

change — but you'll drive yourself crazy and you'll never get a package finished if you keep tweaking it. Don't overthink your copy. Don't fill your mind with self-doubt. And for goodness sake, don't stress yourself out! If you've written solid copy, turn it in and get it tested! The market will ultimately decide if it's a success — not you!

One of my mentors, Bob King used to say, "Be the best part of someone's day."

Imagine when your prospect goes to the mailbox and pulls out your promotion. What he reads might be the highlight of his day. His life may be very monotonous now. Maybe he's 80 years old... living alone... feeling sick and tired of doing the same thing every day.

You have the opportunity to bring sunshine and joy into his life. So what are you going to say to him? Is it...

> "Scientific studies show that 90% of adults over 80 years old suffer from short-term memory loss and blah blah blah..."

Come on — is that really what he wants to hear? Is that going to connect you with this person? Is he really going to think you care about HIM?

But if you tried something like this...

> "Dear Friend, are you worried that you forgot to turn off the oven before you left the house again? Or maybe you recognize the face but the

name is stuck on the tip of your tongue. As you're getting older, are you concerned about being a burden to your children? Do you want to know if there's something you can do right now to save your memory? If so, let me tell you about a new discovery that could possibly help you."

That's the difference between facts and a conversation. When you write to your market — whoever he is — make your copy a highlight of his day. Even if your prospect doesn't order (yet) — give him valuable information that makes him better off for taking the time to read your message.

You may even save his life.

SEVEN

Be Prepared to Eat a Big Ol' Serving of Humble Pie

The direct-response industry has a way of keeping you humble.

No matter how good you are — you're going to fail and you're going to fail a lot. And the success and failure you experience in this industry can feel like whiplash.

For example…

… In ONE day, I had a client call me and tell me my promo got the worst results they've seen in years! I couldn't believe how bad I sucked. And then, about three hours later, another client told me my promo was kicking butt with a nearly 2% response. They couldn't believe the amazing results. Wow — now, I'm awesome! This was the time when I coined the phrase, "I'm Suck-Awesome!"

Getting to be an A-list copywriter doesn't mean you will have a 100% success rate. It doesn't mean all your ideas are great. It doesn't mean you won't get your butt spanked in the mail.

It just means you have more successes than failures.

And that reminds me of one of my favorite Michael Jordan quotes:

> "I've missed more than 9,000 shots in my career. I've lost almost 300 games. 26 times, I've been trusted to take the game winning shot and missed. I've failed over and over and over again in my life. And that is why I succeed."

Babe Ruth was a home run king — and he was also the king of strike-outs. But nobody cares about the latter.

To be successful writing to the 50+ year-old white male market — or any market — you just have to do the best you possibly can. Keep taking the shots. Keep coming up with new ideas. Keep talking to your market about relevant issues. Not everything you write will work — and that's OK. You can be successful just by volume: the more you write, the more likely it is that something's going to work!

And sometimes success may just be out of your control.

What you have to realize is that the copy is only about 20% of the marketing equation. The client also has to mail that copy to the right list — which is about 40% of the equation. And the offer must be strong because that accounts for another 30% of the equation. And that last 10%? I call that 'fluke.' Something weird, crazy or unexpected can totally jack up a mailing and cause your package to fail!

Here are just a few situations that occurred to really screw up results on some of my packages...

- **The client mailed my promo to the wrong mailing list.** It was some crazy computer error from the list broker. The results bombed!
- **The postal facility handling the mailing caught on fire.** My client never knew there was a problem until results tanked. They later discovered that more than half of the mailing quantity went up in smoke. My promo never reached the prospect's mailbox.
- **The mail truck that was supposed to deliver the mailing to specific zip codes flipped over on a major highway.** The contents of the truck — including my promos — were ruined. Again, we didn't find out about this until the results sucked.
- Back in the early 1990s when I worked at Georgetown Publishing House, my boss, Dani Levinas, claimed **the post office was dumping third-class mail** (now called marketing mail) when they were overworked or short-staffed. That accusation made the news and caused a big stir in the industry!

I say all this to remind you that STUFF HAPPENS. But instead of worrying about what's out of your control — focus on what you *can* do. And that's to deliver strong, compelling, creative, out-of-the-box copy to your clients.

And have fun with that copy!

This is a business where you can test some really crazy ideas. Go for it. Some of them will work and a lot of them won't. And that's OK! It will keep you humble.

But you do need to be strategic about your copy tests. Because ultimately your job is to deliver your client a winner. So how do you do that — and still take risks? Well, here's what I do…

… For every package I write, I make sure to have one test cover that I call my 'bread and butter.' This is the 'Momma's gotta pay the mortgage' cover. It may not be pretty or sexy or creative — but it's going to be a solid test. I may just state the benefit… or the USP… or put a great offer on the cover. Again, it's not sexy — but it's got a low-risk, high-success potential. Once I nail down that cover…

… I GO FOR IT!

Now I'm just going to have some fun. I think to myself, *"What's the craziest thing I can think of for this product?"* These ideas may not work, but if they do — WHOAH! Using this process has helped me to get solid controls — and still create some wacky covers that sometimes work like gangbusters. For example…

… I was hired to write a launch package for a heart supplement called 'Peak Cardio Platinum.' It contained nutrients that cleared calcium plaque out of arteries, boosted nitric oxide production and energized the heart.

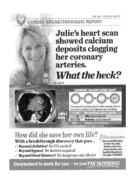

So my 'bread and butter' approach was to show how just about everyone over 50 has clogged arteries.

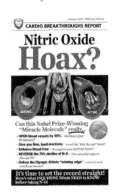

After that, I started taking risks. I called the whole nitric oxide movement a hoax.

And then I went really crazy by telling stories of folks who beat near-death experiences…

The winner?

In this case — 'bread and butter' prevailed! *Julie's Heart Scan* was the winner. However…

The *Nitric Oxide Hoax* was also powerful enough to become a second control. Once the *Julie's Heart Scan* cover began to fatigue — the client switched to the *Nitric Oxide Hoax* cover. The client rotated the mailings

between these two covers for over two years.

The *Heart Tales* cover — which actually gave me the original idea for the entire theme of the promo — TANKED! It was my 'GO FOR IT' cover — and I struck out! I loved that cover but I covered my butt by offering my 50+ year-old white male market different options. The mailing would've flopped if that was the only cover I gave to my client.

Even if I know mentally that I'm taking risks that may not pay off — it still feels like a punch in the gut when NONE of my cover tests work. The Imposter Syndrome still creeps back into my head. I feel like I must have just been a fake copywriter for the last 21 years! I start thinking, *"Have I lost it? Am I ever going to get another control? Does everybody now know that I really do suck?"*

When a client calls me and says my package bombed, I'll say, "OK, give me the results... let me call you back."

Then I hang up the phone... and cry like a girl.

I used to call Clayton, saying "I suck, I suck! I don't know what I did wrong! I'm never going to get another job again." And he would just let me ramble on and on until I could hear how stupid I sounded.

Man, I miss those conversations with him.

And I'd also call my husband and say, "I'm a failure.

I need ice cream! A pint of Pralines 'n' Cream — no, make it a quart size. I need it now, please!"

It's like a mourning process. I spent a month of my life on a project that didn't work. So I go through this pity party — and then I get back to work. I call up the client and discuss the next step. If he's willing to re-test, I will rewrite the package at no additional cost.

I'll go back and study the promo: Was my headline targeted enough? Should I try a new lead? Did I have enough proof elements? What new cover tests can I come up with? I'll even reach out to a fellow copywriter and ask him or her to crit the copy for me. I want the dang thing to WIN!

Now, my clients know there are so many things that can kill a mailing. They're not coming back to me saying, "Hey Carline, you suck!" That's ME feeling that way. But I want a winner and clients are usually willing to try again.

And oftentimes, we'll end up with a revised package that now *spanks* the control.

It might be an idea that even I thought was too crazy! Sometimes the cover has nothing to do with the product... nothing to do with the inside copy... but it's just a zany idea that grabs the prospect's attention — and gets them inside to read more! For example…

Take a look at this:

With a cover like that — wouldn't you assume the copy inside is talking about CBD? I sure would. But the truth is: the inside copy doesn't talk about CBD at all. This was a last-minute test idea to jump on the

CBD bandwagon when it was hot. We didn't have time for a new lead or any changes to the inside copy to tie in this CBD idea. But if you read the deck copy closely,

Your cover doesn't HAVE to reflect the internal copy

you'll see I'm not talking about CBD at all. I'm teasing a 3,000-year-old sacred oil that's saving lives! And that's what the inside copy is about.

This cover beat the control and gave new life to the package! Crazy — but true story! I've used this approach several times to test a new idea on the cover before

rewriting the inside copy. You may want to try it too.

So — what really counts as a success when it comes to mailing a direct-response package?

If I came home from school with a B, my Mom would think I was slacking off. If I got a C — a 70% grade — I was in trouble. I wouldn't even come home if my grade was a D or lower! So it's pretty ironic that I work in an industry where a 1% response makes me a success… and a 2% response makes me a genius!

Young writers are floored when I tell them that 99% of the people who receive their promotions in the mail will NOT respond. That's just how this crazy business operates. So take it in stride. Have as much fun as you can when you're working on your sales pieces. Yes, sometimes stuff fails and that sucks — but it's OK. Your promo sucked. You don't.

Learn To Shut Your Pie Hole!

One of the most important skills for a copywriter is the ability to shut your pie hole.

It's hard, because you're very passionate about what you're doing and you're very invested in your work. So it sucks to have somebody come in — a copy chief or a client — and just start crossing out copy you think is great.

I get it! You feel like you've given them your best — and when the edits come back, you're looking at a sea of red ink, barely able to find an original sentence or word.

But the best way to grow and sharpen your skills is for someone experienced to rip your copy to shreds. If you find that person — shut your pie hole and listen to what that A-level writer is telling you. It doesn't matter whether you agree with the crits or not. If they're a working copywriter, they are taking away valuable time from working on their copy to help you with yours. So take a healthy dose of shut-the-heck-up!

I quickly learned that whenever Clayton Makepeace made me cry, my income increased.

Clayton was brutal with his copy crits. He just zoned into the copy and found the problem spots. He didn't have time to worry about hurting my feelings. It was about getting the copy right. If the copy was lame

— he showed me how to strengthen it. If I got off track — he kicked my butt into gear. If I wasn't focusing on my 50+ year-old white male market — he told me to "put on your big girl pants and write like a man!"

Yep, many times he hurt my feelings and yes, sometimes I cried. Then I fixed the copy and I usually got a winner.

I can be tough on my copy cubs too. I'm definitely tough on clients who want me to consult for them about copy. I look at it this way: I charge a $2,500 hourly consulting fee. And payment is due before we even start the discussion. So I begin the meeting by saying something like this:

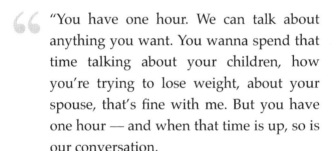

"You have one hour. We can talk about anything you want. You wanna spend that time talking about your children, how you're trying to lose weight, about your spouse, that's fine with me. But you have one hour — and when that time is up, so is our conversation.

So, in order to maximize your hour, my recommendation is that you ask a question — and let me answer it. Take all the crits you can get. It won't hurt my feelings if you don't follow through on anything I suggest. But at least hear me out by not interrupting or making excuses for your copy. If you follow these guidelines, I promise you're going to get

more than your money's worth during
this hour."

It's really difficult for most writers to take this
advice.

I'll say, "You're burying your lead..." and before I
know it, the writer is cutting me off to explain his
thought process and why he took this approach. So I
let him ramble on for 10 minutes. When he's done, I
just pick up where I was interrupted: "Like I said,
you're burying your lead..." His explanation doesn't
change my opinion — but he's lost 10 minutes of the
hour.

When you're getting crits, you don't need to justify
your copy. Let the copy be judged on its own merits.
Make sure you turn in the best copy you can write —
and let the experienced copywriter help you make it
even stronger.

For example, one of my cubs (I'll call him Brad...
because that's his name) was working on a blood pressure product. He did a good job gathering the information but his copy was just sentence, sentence, sentence
and sentence.

I said, "Dude! Take all those sentences and tell me a
story! You've got great facts — but none of them are
connecting with one another, you're not giving me a
thread to hold on to. Make those facts come alive with a
great story."

Then I showed him how to do it. I didn't add
anything new to what he wrote — all I did was person-

alize it. He listened. And went to work. His next draft was light-years better!

I tell my writers:

> "When you send me your copy, I am going to sit on my hands. My goal is to read your copy like I just received it in the mail. If I have to take my hands from under my butt and start making changes, there's a problem."

If I can sit on my hands and the copy keeps me interested — congratulations! But if your copy is giving me whiplash because you're jerking me from one thought to another — you're not done, no matter how many drafts you've written.

Here's what I tell my copy cubs to do and I can always tell when they don't follow this advice:

Read your copy out loud and listen to how it sounds.

If it doesn't sound like you're having a conversation, then you're just writing words. Go back and turn it into a conversation. It's OK to start sentences with a "But…" or an "And…" or "Did you know…" or, "Huh! What do you think about that?"

Add those little quirks and nuances we use in everyday speech.

Listen to your copy.

Better still — hire a 10 year-old to read your copy to you. See where he stumbles. See where he has to repeat a sentence again because he didn't understand what the heck it was saying. Those are the places your reader may get stuck too!

And remember: the goal of writing your copy is to get the client a control. It's not to boost your ego.

A lot of cubs turn in what I call 'warm-up copy.' They take too long to get to the point! So I will usually cut one or two pages from the lead before I get to anything that's really worth reading.

It reminds me of my childhood days playing Double Dutch jump-rope. My cousins Darnelle, Regina, Moon, Pat and Shortie could jump right in and straddle both ropes.

Me?

I would be getting ready to jump in. I wanted to jump in! But I just kept hesitating, afraid to take the leap. My cousins would complain that their arms were getting tired from turning the ropes so long, but I just kept waiting and waiting for the right moment to jump in. And when I finally did — THUD! I stepped on the rope!

That's what warm-up copy is like.

"I'm going in there! I'm gonna do it! It's about to happen! Just you wait!"

But it takes so long that when you finally get to the point — THUD! Your prospect has lost interest!

You Gotta Push The Limits!

Whenever I work with a new client, I try to figure out his 'comfort level' on a scale of 1 to 10 — a 1 being a total scaredy cat about trying new or risky ideas and a 10 being a total maniac who scares ME!

Now, I wanna work with clients who are at least a level 6 or 7 on that scale. That allows me the opportunity to push the creative boundaries to get a winner. You have to take risks and it's important my client knows what I'm going to do from the very beginning.

So if my client has a comfort level of 7 — I'm going to write copy that's at an 8 or a 9. That way, if the client wants me to tone down the promo — I can still end up at a level 7. If I gave him a level 7 at the beginning, it may end up at a level 5 after legal reviews and crits.

Sometimes clients find out they're more willing to take a risk when they see the copy already written for them. So I try to take them outside their comfort zone, because that's where new opportunities for growth are waiting — and where the magic happens!

Now, if there's a part of the copy where the client thinks I went overboard, he can mark it up and I can make the edits. To me, it's much easier to tone down a sales piece than to rev it up.

And I never let the legal department make my changes. They can identify problem areas and bring them to my attention. It's my job to change the copy — not theirs! I tell them I won't give them legal advice and I don't want them to write my copy!

Am I sounding like a 2 year-old, saying, "Mine, mine, mine"?

Well, that's because I'm very possessive of my copy. If I'm taking ownership of the final product — I need to maintain ownership of the process (and I'll tell you more about that in Chapter 10!). I spent too many years of my early career changing my copy based on the client's feedback... and regretting it later. When I deviated from what I really felt was the right approach and started incorporating everybody's ideas, I ended up with a zebra — not a racehorse.

You don't write great copy by committee.

So if you're going to mess with my copy — you better have a good reason!

You'll Always Be My Friend... Because You Know Where The Bodies Are Buried!

There's nothing like traveling to new places to spark creativity and keep you grounded and humble.

Now that my kids are grown, I'm traveling even more — and taking my reluctant travel partner husband with me. In the past few years, we've been invited as delegates to International Conventions of Jehovah's Witnesses in South Africa, Madagascar and South Korea. Plus, we've vacationed in Kenya, Sri Lanka, Mexico, Italy, Ireland, France and Spain — just to name a few.

I'm very thankful to have the opportunity and the means to take these amazing vacations. I am well aware that many people do not have the circumstances or financial means to take these trips. I'm very grateful and I try to learn as much as I can from these amazing experiences.

Travel opens your eyes and really makes you appreciate what you have. So many people around the world don't have squat compared to what you possess right now. Travel shows me that I can live with very little. It's taught me that if everything I own right now disappeared, if copywriting vanished tomorrow, I would be OK as long as I had what really matters: My faith. My family. My friends.

I mean, when we went to Kenya, we stayed in a dung house — yes, a house made of feces. I thought it was ironic that I've had tremendous success writing about bowel health — and now the 'Queen of Poop' is living in a house of dung!

We lived, ate and played with the Maasai tribesmen. Mealtime was very interesting to say the least. Big ol' dragonflies would fall into our bowls. And you had two choices: pluck 'em out... or consider them a protein treat! I got tired of scooping them out of my bowl — and just went for it!

We saw how differently people lived... and how happy they were. They got up when the sun rose and went to bed when it was dark. No alarm clocks. No traffic. No overtime. They took care of their families, worked hard and had fun. It really gave me a clearer perspective on my priorities.

And that perspective is why I cherish my long-term friendships too.

Sure, most of my friends STILL don't know what I do for a living.

I've heard them tell people... "Oh, Carline? She

writes books. No, she copyrights stuff. Oh wait — I think she works at a vitamin store."

I don't bother correcting them anymore. It doesn't matter anyway. I don't know what most of them do for a living either.

What really matters is that when we get together we have fun! I also can trust them to be honest with me — we keep it real! They know when I start off a sentence with, "You know I love you, right?" that they're going to hear something they may not like, but it's gotta be said because I truly love them.

We've been through the trenches together. Experienced losses and disappointments. Shared maternity and kids clothes. And we were broke — and I mean *broke*, no kidding. We got each other through some very difficult times. Those friends are extremely important to me and they keep me humble. Many of those friendships have lasted over 40 years and I'm extremely proud of that. I have a magnet on my refrigerator that says, *"You'll always be my friend, because you know where the bodies are buried!"*

EIGHT

How My Four Kids Taught Me Valuable Lessons in Copywriting!

There's only one thing I love more than motherhood…

… And that's grandmotherhood!

Being "Coco" to my grandsons Dallas, Carson, Maverick and Colton gives me all the best parts of being a mom — without the work. Love that!

I have a sign in my family room that says, *"If I had known grandkids would be this much fun — I would've had them FIRST!"*

But before I got to enjoy my golden years of grandmotherhood — I definitely had to pay my dues as a mom. But my four kids Milan, Tiara, Jael and Chadam were the best gifts my husband ever gave me. I could not imagine my life without them. They helped me grow as a human being, woman and mom. Plus — they taught me some valuable copywriting lessons I still use today to write kick-butt copy!

Four Different Kids, Four Different Lessons!

Who'd a thunk that being a mom would be the secret to becoming a million-dollar copywriter?

After all, I had no idea what copywriting was about when I was squeezing out my puppies. But you know what? Each of those four VERY different personalities taught me important lessons in identifying and catering to my 50+ year-old white male market.

Because my kids are SO different — Mick and I had to customize our parenting skills to target their personalities. A 'one size fits all' approach simply would not work.

If you're familiar with the Myers–Briggs personality tests, we were raising an ESTJ, an ENFJ, an ISFP and an ISTJ. And Mick is an ESTP and I'm an over-the-top ENFP. If you're not familiar with Myers–Briggs — just know this: We're dealing with LOTS of personality clashes here!

We weren't trying to raise robots. We wanted to raise good human beings with their own special talents. But for each kid to develop her or his best potential — we had to find the best approach to address their needs.

Writing good copy is very similar.

When you're working on a project — you've got to find what really works. You need to identify your market's dominant emotions. And you need to present the offer in a way that's understandable so your prospect can take action. In other words…

… You've got to figure out what makes your

prospect tick, so you can get him to do what you want. Each of my kids gave me insight on how to tap into my market in very unique ways.

KID #1: THE SKEPTIC

Daughter #1 is still my most skeptical child. Don't say anything to her unless you can back it up. She's not going to trust you until you've proven to be trustworthy. And growing up, that kid had a serious attitude! In a nutshell, she was my "so what?" kid.

You couldn't just tell her what to do — you had to give her a reason why. For example...

... If I said to this 3 year-old, "Put your toys away, please" — I may have to say it (or threaten her with punishment) several times before she would act.

But if I said, "Put your toys away so you can go outside and play," I got much better results. That brief extra explanation made all the difference in the world.

A 'do this' approach very seldom worked. But a 'do this *because*...' approach oftentimes succeeded.

If you couldn't convince her — she would dig in her heels and wouldn't budge. But if you spent the time to explain *why* and she understood the authority behind the request — then confrontations were often avoided. So our conversations would go something like this...

"If you do this, then that is going to happen... and then this will be the consequence. How do I know? Well, I've been through this before. I have experience — you don't. So I need you to trust me on this because..."

'Because' is a very powerful word.

Because you will break your leg.

Because you will be grounded.

Because you will die.

Adding 'because' in conversations with this kid made a huge difference. And it really didn't matter what the 'because' was. And yes, I frequently said, *"Because I'm your mother, that's why!"*

I keep this 'so what?' skeptical attitude in mind when I'm talking to my 50+ year-old white male market too. He doesn't know my product or my guru. So why should he trust me? I can't just tell him what to do until I've given him proof that I can deliver the goods.

I've got to give him solid evidence from scientific studies, research from credible sources and even testimonials that show that other people have experienced success with this product. And then I have to tell him WHY.

There's a great study in one of my favorite books, *Yes: 50 Scientifically Proven Ways to Be Persuasive* by Noah J. Goldstein, Robert Cialdini and Steve Martin. It really sealed it in my brain to make sure I explain my reasoning to my prospect. It also confirms the power of 'because.'

The study took place in an office where people were waiting in line to use the copy machine — remember those days?

The researchers would send someone to go to the front of the long line and say, "Excuse me, may I cut in front of you?" Then they monitored how many times the person received a yes or no response.

Then the researchers would send someone else to the front of the long line, but this person was instructed to say, "May I cut in front of you because I just need to make a few copies?"

Now — what is everyone in that line trying to do? Make copies, right? But when the person added a 'because' to their request — even if the reason was trivial — he was twice as likely to get a "yes."

Yep! The response rate doubled when the prospect was given a reason why.

And it turned out that giving just about any reason was more effective than no reason at all:

- "Because I only need to make two copies"
- "Because I'm in a hurry"
- "Because I have to go to the hairdresser."

Just saying "because…" and giving a reason why increased the response rate!

Wow! Isn't that a powerful tool for a direct-response writer? I sure think so!

Without a reason, people naturally feel skeptical and want to know *why*. So if you make sure to provide that reason in your copy, you reduce resistance. And that's why you'll find the word 'because' in my copy A LOT!

Daughter #1's skepticism also taught me how to get better information out of my clients. I use that 'so what?' attitude when I meet with them. I make my client justify why I should spend a month of my life working on his product. This is really powerful and here's why...

... If I've asked the right questions during my client meeting, I can uncover the theme of my package before the meeting is over.

I ask the client...

- "What's so great about this product?"
- "Why is your brand better than your competitors?"
- "Would I want my Mom to take this stuff?"
- "What's in it — and why?"
- "How can you prove it works?"
- "Who else thinks this formula is great?"

I'm extremely skeptical in that meeting, because at that moment, I'm not the copywriter. I'm the customer. If the client can't convince me his product is good — then why should I try to convince anybody else?

By the time this meeting is done, the client has usually given me several ideas for cover tests and themes. Many times, the client has practically talked out the entire sales package — and now all I have to do is put it down in writing!

So make sure to use 'reason why' copy to satisfy your skeptical market. Here's an approach Clayton Makepeace taught me — and I still use it often today. Towards the close of the sale — I give my prospects a bunch of reasons why they need to say YES to this invitation...

In this conclusion — I actually give 9 reasons why the customer needs to act now!

Remember this: If you give your prospect a reason why – he'll have no reason not to buy!

KID #2: THE DRAMA QUEEN

"And the Academy Award goes to..."

That's what I think when Daughter #2 starts to tell me about her trials and tribulations. This kid is a drama queen!

Life is a stage and she's the star.

Now — place the back of your right hand on your forehead... add in some heavy sighs... and you'll start to get a visual of this kid in action.

Her throat is not sore… "It's on FIRE! The pain is unbearable — I can hardly talk, let alone breathe! Oh Mother, I'm going to DIE!"

She's not tired… "I'm so EXHAUSTED — can you please help me to the chair, I don't have the energy… oh, I feel faint, I'm going to pass out!"

It's not just a nice gift… "It's the BEST, most THOUGHTFUL present ANYONE has EVER given me in my WHOLE entire LIFE!"

She lives in her own world — a place where you open the windows in the morning and the bluebirds come out with a wreath of flowers for your hair and serenade you… the sun shines on your face while little mice help you get dressed… and there's a prince on a white horse just waiting to come and sweep you off your feet!

I love her world!

Daughter #2 is my reminder to add some drama and some flair to my copy!

Remember — what you're writing may be the highlight of someone's day. You're in the 'infotainment' business. Nobody's going to read your copy unless you make it interesting and worth their while. So — let the production begin!

Set the scene. Who's your hero? Where's the villain? What's the setting? Where's the controversy? What's the resolution? You've got to keep your reader hooked all the way to the order form!

You're not just writing copy — you're creating an experience and developing a great story.

Sometimes the story will be happy… other times it will be sad or downright scary. And that's OK — just take the reader along for the ride!

I'm a long-form copywriter. That means my reader is receiving a promotion that's 20 or 30 pages in length. He doesn't have to read my stuff. He didn't invite me into his mailbox. So I've got to stop him dead in his tracks — and MAKE him want to read more!

I want my reader to squirm. I want him to laugh. I want him to cry. I want to tap as many emotional buttons I possibly can as he's reading my story. I want him to ask, "What happens next?" I want him to have no other choice but to turn the page and keep reading to find out!

Then I want to reward him for reading by making sure he's learned something valuable during our time together. And then I want to give him an amazing opportunity that's only available right now — for a limited time only! And then I want him to ACT to pick up that phone and CALL NOW to claim his FREE gifts!

You can do all that and more when you tell a great story and treat your copy like a production number! Add that drama and flair whenever you can!

Start the story on the cover… or make the story part of your lead!

KID #3: THE BRICK WALL

Daughter #3 has one of the most difficult person-ality types for someone like me to parent. I'm emotional… passionate… enthusiastic. But this kid doesn't give a squat about squat! She doesn't react — good or bad — about anything!

You took away her toys. Alright.

You sent her to her room. Whatever.

You tell her no TV. Who cares?

You buy her brand new Nikes? Thanks.

You take her to Disney World? OK.

Her apathy drove me nuts! She gave me no reaction — so I couldn't figure out what was going on in her brain. Give me extreme hatred, give me extreme love — I can handle either one, but man, apathy — that was her superpower.

The few times we were able to get a reaction out of her, I nearly had a heart attack! (Sorry — that was totally a Daughter #2 comment. Now you know where SHE gets it from!)

It took me a long time to realize that what we thought was apathy was really a form of self-protection.

When she was little, between the ages of 3 and 7 — she would get very sick with a respiratory illness. A minor cold would quickly turn into a breathing crisis. Those years, we spent nearly every winter in the ICU. Her lungs collapsed several times. She was even transported by medevac because her condition had gotten so bad. Those were scary times.

At one point, doctors thought she possibly had cystic fibrosis. They tried all sorts of medications to keep her lungs open. It wasn't until much later that I discovered some of those drugs could affect learning — especially when given to children in their formative years.

So she struggled in school. For this kid a C was a great grade. If she got a B, we were ready to throw a party, but she didn't care about that! Things didn't come easy for her and she started using apathy as a means of self-protection.

When she was asked a question, she wouldn't answer. That way you wouldn't know if she was right or wrong — she couldn't be wrong if she didn't try at all. But many times she couldn't answer because she didn't understand the question properly. When the question was rephrased or explained, she could give a correct reply.

When I picked up on that, I realized I had to keep

things simple. Break stuff down in smaller chunks. Add some cues with step-by-step instructions. Give her time to process. And then she'd get it. Instead of rushing through instructions, I had to slow down and make sure she was still with me every step of the way.

She was such a powerful inspiration to me.

When I write copy — Daughter #3 helps me remember that I can't rush my copy. I can't assume my 50+ year-old white male prospect will understand what I'm saying. I need to take him by the hand on this journey and make sure I don't lose him with big words or complicated thoughts. I need to keep it simple. Make it relevant. Keep him engaged.

I have to grab him by the eyeballs with a strong headline. Keep his attention with a powerful story. And let him know he can trust me with a strong and powerful guarantee.

And when I have to talk about a hard-to-pronounce nutrient— like phosphatidylserine — I make it easy for him to get it — by saying something like this...

 *Dear Friend,*

> *It's pronounced: "**foss-fah-tie-doll-sir-een**"... but if you're experiencing memory loss... age-related memory decline... fuzzy thinking... 'senior moments'... mental confusion... or brain aging — you're going to call it a **Godsend**! Why? Because phosphatidylserine — or "**PS**" for short — is Nature's Amazing Brain Saver!*

I may even simplify it further by saying that phosphatidylserine is just *"a fancy-schmancy word for a nutrient that makes your brain cells come alive..."*

I do that a lot. I don't want to risk losing my reader because he doesn't understand what I'm talking about! Nobody wants to feel dumb — help your prospect understand, so he sticks with you.

I'm not trying to impress anybody with my copy. I don't care who the doctor or guru is, he's still going to speak at a fifth-grade level or lower.

That way, if the person reading the copy has a college degree, he'll understand — and so will the guy with a fifth-grade education!

I don't do snooty.

Apathy happens when you haven't made it worthwhile for your reader to care. And that will get your promo trashed. Your job is to engage your reader. You can do that by keeping your message simple, focused and interesting.

Make it easy for the prospect to order the product.

Use calls to action such as "Call TOLL FREE 1-800-XXX-XXXX throughout your copy.

Remember this: K.I.S.S! Keep it simple, sweetie!

KID #4: THE CLOWN

My #4 kid and my only son, is my clown. He reminds me that if you're not laughing at least 20 times a day — something's wrong.

And if you can't find a way to make other people smile or laugh — then something's wrong with you.

It's funny because he's actually an introvert. I call him my sneaky clown, because he's a quiet guy — you don't expect any shenanigans... and then BAM! He catches you off guard. For example...

... When he was graduating from Rocky Hill Middle School, he was going to receive an award for Outstanding Citizenship. But the week before the ceremonies, he got suspended from school for setting off firecrackers. I was so mad at him. When I asked, "What were you thinking?" He replied, "We were just having some fun, Mom. No one got hurt." So while someone *else* received the Outstanding Citizenship award — he was 'out standing' in the backyard doing his sisters' chores as a punishment!

But my son reminds me that at the end of the day — if you've had fun, you probably had a good day.

That's why I try to include some fun in my copy too. If I can get my reader to laugh out loud — or even chuckle — I've got his attention and I'm closer to nailing the sale.

So try to use humor to get your point across. Try it on a cover test like this…

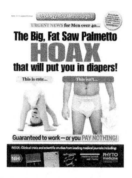

Designer Rob Davis took this cover to a whole new level! Love it — and it was a control for years!

Or this…

Designer Rick Thayne took an embarrassing moment — and made the reader laugh.

Once when I was working on an anti-inflammatory

turmeric supplement, I had an idea for a cartoon. In the first frame, someone is holding an ad that shows a bowl of turmeric. The text in the ad reads: *"Turmeric! The Golden Indian Spice. Great for Inflammation! Try It Today."*

In the next frame, you see a pair of legs running along, with the caption: *"Carly's knees starting to feel better..."* In the final frame, we see a very orange Carly running along. *"But now she wonders if she's taking <u>too</u> much turmeric?"*

Cartoonist Troy Jensen had fun showing how powerful the Golden Spice Turmeric can be.

Have fun using humor in your copy. Add a quiz. Try a puzzle, or tell a joke — just be careful of off-color jokes that can backfire on you!

Don't take yourself or your copy too seriously. If your reader sees you as a regular guy — it can make your copy even stronger!

The "Pick Your Poo" quiz kept this promo a control for over five years.

Cartoons can help readers understand complicated ideas.

And it's OK to show you're human. Say something like, *"Frankly, I had no idea what he was talking about, until I..."* It helps the reader connect with you and feel relaxed.

That's really important!

There's also an element of surprise in humor that keeps readers engaged. When you can surprise your reader in your copy, you keep him on the edge of his seat. He's not sure what you're going to say or do next — and that's exciting! So use visual words — like 'KABOOM... HOGWASH... HOLEY MOLEY' — and other energy-filled words to make your point!

Reading your copy shouldn't feel like work.

That's why using short sentences and varying the length is important.

I'll have a paragraph that contains just a sentence or a word.

One.

Then I follow it up with a paragraph containing just two or three sentences. That's it.

These strategies help keep your copy momentum strong.

Avoid big blocks of copy — unless you absolutely don't want your prospect to read it. I'll intentionally use large copy blocks when I have to show legal disclaimers. In this case, I *want* that copy to look unappealing, hard-to-read and boring.

You can make your copy fun by throwing in some quotes from noted experts. It's also OK to interrupt your thought with something completely different. We do that all the time when we speak. So do it in your copy, too. For example — start making a statement and then interrupt yourself with a, "More on that later, but first…"

When I would kiss Kid #4 goodnight at bedtime, I would ask him if he had fun that day. Usually he had a smile on his face and said "Yes — and I'm going to have MORE fun tomorrow!"

That's your goal as a copywriter too. Add more fun to each of your writing projects — and make each one better than the last! Don't deprive your reader of the opportunity to have some fun for the day!

Speaking of depriving someone of fun — this

reminds me of the day I told my 5 year-old grandson Maverick that I had a surprise for him. When I handed him the big bag — he was smiling from ear to ear. He couldn't wait to tear into that bag. He opened it up and started pulling out shirts, pants, suits, all kinds of clothes. When he got to the bottom of the bag, his face completely changed. He looked at me and said, "Coco, these are clothes. They are not fun. TOYS are fun."

I cracked up laughing. But he was right. Even though his parents were thrilled they didn't have to buy a winter wardrobe — clothes aren't fun to a 5 year-old boy. I should've stuck a toy surprise at the bottom of that bag!

So figure out what your market needs to have fun — and deliver it in your copy.

NINE

Copy is King... but Design is His Queen

I would not be successful in this biz if it weren't for my amazing designers. They're the Robin to my Batman. Because the truth is, no matter how great your copy is — if it's not readable, it won't work.

Notice I said 'readable' and not 'designed.' That's because a well-designed sales promo isn't really 'designed' — it supports the copy. It keeps the prospect reading. It leads him to the order page. Now: the sales copy may look fancy, fun or really cool — but that's not the main purpose. The goal is to support the copy.

And that's the difference between a graphic designer and a direct-response graphic designer.

Many graphic designers want to create something beautiful. A direct-response graphic designer knows ugly is also powerful.

That's because the purpose of the design is to appeal to my 50+ year-old white male market in ways that will make him stop and pay attention to what I have to say.

Showcase my headline. Bring the reader INSIDE the sales piece — and keep him reading!

Now, don't get me wrong — I'm not saying direct-response graphic designers aren't creative folks. The ones I work with are extremely creative. But they're keenly aware their job is to help me nail the sale. And like I said earlier, sometimes a simple, low-key, or even ugly design may be the direction it takes to get a winner!

Direct-response designers understand how to use call-to-action devices, such as, *"Pick up the phone now — and Call 1-800-xxx-xxxx to claim your FREE gifts NOW!"* They know how to draw the eye of the reader to certain points in the copy. They know how to enhance the reader's experience… create interest… suspense… and even shock!

They will intentionally break the copy mid-sentence at the end of a page...

… Because they know the brain wants closure. So if it's an incomplete sentence — the brain will force those fingers to TURN THE PAGE and find out what happened to the rest of that sentence.

They put breathing space on the page so the reader isn't looking at a dense wall of copy that feels overwhelming to read.

They leave their ego at the door and focus on making the design work for the copy — not vice versa. And like I said — sometimes this can mean delivering a simple, low-key, ugly design that makes the copy shine.

One of my favorite designers, Lori Haller, calls this

"good ugly". She started using that term after testing so many beautiful covers against ugly ones — and the ugly ones oftentimes won!

So... What Does Good Direct-Response Design Actually Look Like?

Instead of trying to explain design from a copywriter's perspective — I decided to let a pro give it to you straight. Lori is one of the all-time greats with over 20 years of experience in direct-response design. So I asked her to share her view of the role of a direct-response designer...

 "The most important part of being a direct-response designer is understanding who I'm talking to so that I can work out how to get their attention.

Most design schools teach you to create beautiful, magnificent designs. But the one important piece that's missing is that beautiful design often doesn't actually speak to your audience.

In my agency we're continuously studying behavioral science and psychology. Understanding human behavior is just so critical — we're not just studying the fonts, the colors, or a particular style of design.

It's those feelings and psychological

behaviors you really need to dig deeply into.

Designers are like wizards, leading readers all over the campaign... we want to make them interact and really get deeply involved in the copy. Design can help pull together a person's deepest feelings and bring them to the forefront.

Let's say, for example, that I'm working on a joint pain package.

I'll put myself into the reader's mind long before I start thinking about the design itself: *I'm in my 60s, I used to play a lot of sports when I was younger, so now I have terrible joint pain. It keeps me from sleeping well at night. I can't pick up my granddaughter anymore. I feel like I'm losing my youth and I can't do the things I want to, which is very emotionally painful on top of all the physical pain.*

So I know that in a package like that, I don't want to use a lot of red. Red conjures up pain, danger, alertness — I want to use soothing blues and healthy greens to put them at ease, to build trust and to lead them to look at the bottle, which might be bright white, clinical and authoritative in style.

Your designer should understand all

this and how to draw the eye of the reader to keep them engaged.

Readability is king, so we also need to choose a friendly, easy-to-read font. We want to make sure the spacing between paragraphs is properly considered as well.

You want to give the reader just enough space between a paragraph or line of copy to understand what he's just read, breathe and go to the next section.

But you don't want to add too much space and give him a chance to stop reading the copy.

Subheads should be big and easy to read. They often have a contrasting color and along with highlights within the text, are intended to carry the reader down the page.

Images have captions, so the 'skimmers' who don't read the whole text still understand what's happening.

The images themselves — along with charts and photographs — visually represent what's happening in the copy too.

You want to lead your prospect to a crescendo at the end — to make sure your audience knows exactly what they're going to receive with the offer and to give them as many opportunities to say 'yes' as possible.

And when considering design for print, the front and back covers of a campaign are absolutely crucial. Most designers leave those for last and rush them, but they're what you should actually begin with!

If we can't convince the reader to open the package after looking at the covers, they're never going to see all of the important internal copy and design — even if it's the best thing you've ever created.

You should have a very specific idea of the different kinds of readers you will have and create cover elements that appeal to every one of them.

All these different elements are strategically designed to hold the reader on the page. They keep the reader from getting bored or distracted. We have to entertain them, build trust and educate them.

It's the duty of the designer to make the reader stick to the page, to help them get through a long piece of copy and to be able to put deep trust into the product or service. In the end, the goal is to make them feel like they simply can't live another day without what's being offered."

Thanks Lori — I'd say that gives you a good idea of what goes on in an A-list designer's mind!

How To Get Kick-Butt Designs — My Process

I can't tell you how many times I've seen mediocre copy kick butt simply because it's well-designed. And on the flipside — I've seen killer copy bomb because the design sabotaged the copy. The bad design either distracted the reader with unnecessary bells and whistles — or failed to direct him through the copy.

That's why I stay very much a part of the design process, from beginning to end.

If I'm working with a designer for the first time — I make sure he's a direct-response designer — not just a graphic designer. It's sad that some clients still don't understand this big difference.

When the copy is finished and has gone through legal review, I'll have a kickoff meeting with my designer. If I have a specific vision in mind, I'll communicate that to him. I don't want my designer to start working on the package without this initial conversation. It saves lots of time — and cuts down on the number of drafts — if we can talk first.

I don't think it's fair to simply hand off a package to the designer and expect him to come up with the perfect idea. This is teamwork — and you want to give your designer the best opportunity to succeed. So if you're looking for a low-key design or a 'go for it' crazy idea — you need to convey that message to the designer as early as possible.

Now, you don't need to have every specific detail pinned down, but in the kick-off meeting, you should be able to give your designer a sense of how you see the package turning out. Again — it will save lots of headaches down the road.

Even before I'm assigned a designer — I'm already thinking about design ideas as I write my copy. I'm dropping in notes and making suggestions as I write headlines, lead and sidebars. I'll even find stock photos and medical logos I want used — and drop them in my Word doc. If I'm typing away and envisioning something specific, I'll add a note into the text so the designer can follow along with me. I'll just put a bracket with a note, like... *[DESIGN: Give this a scientific feel]*.

By the time I'm finished writing the package — I've got LOTS of notes for my designer!

One of the most important lessons I've learned from working with my amazing designers is to be as clear as possible in my copy. In other words...

... Don't trip up your designer!

Write the copy so your designer understands what goes where and why.

I once interviewed Rob Davis — another one of my all-time favorite designers (and the creative genius who designed the cover for this book!) about his pet peeves working with copywriters. He told me that sometimes he receives copy that's just a big wall of text — he has no idea what the headline is... where subheads start... or which pieces of copy belong in the sidebars.

Yikes, what a nightmare!

Here's what else Rob told me in that interview...

> "Great copywriters give great direction. Giving me some indication on where you want the sidebars to go in the copy, for example, is exactly the kind of direction I like to see.
>
> I want to know what you consider to be an important concept. Some elements are more important than others, so if I know what you think is important, it helps me a lot to get the design right the first time around.
>
> If I have to guess what's important, we're going to waste a lot of time rearranging pieces that need to do a particular job in the copy."

So make it easy for your designer and yourself:

- **Show the headline with a bold font in a large size.** I like Impact font in 24 point or larger.
- **Make the subheads bold and clear on their own line.** I also center my subheads.

- **Identify sidebars.** I keep mine all together in a clearly-identified section in the Word doc called [SIDEBARS]. I number each one and make a note of roughly where it should appear in the package.
- **Identify all the elements in the piece.** For example: [Pub Note], [Testimonials], [Doc Bio], etc…
- **Identify any copy you want highlighted in yellow or written in a handwriting font.** A few of these treatments really makes the page POP!

Following these simple tips can make working with your designer much easier — and can help you meet or beat deadlines!

But remember this: while you don't relinquish control of the copy — you do have to allow the designer to take some ownership at this stage. This is his time to shine. He's the expert at this stage. So while I give LOTS of comments throughout my copy — my designers know that all my notes come with the caveat that they are just design *suggestions.*

The designers I work with are A-level. They've been in the business a long time. I'm not a designer and I don't want to play one on TV either! Just like I don't want somebody telling me how to write my copy — I don't want to tell the designer how to do his job.

Yes, we will battle it out if we strongly disagree. But I've learned to listen and if it's a better idea — I shut my pie hole and go with it. Many times I've had a great idea for a design... my designer came up with something completely different... and it worked! Again — this is teamwork. So respect each other's creativity and ability.

The one thing I demand from my designers — whenever possible — is to use people of color in the design. If I don't see them in the first draft, he's going to get a, "Hey — where are the black people?" email from me. And I don't mean shoving a tiny photo in the back of the promo as an afterthought either!

Yes — it's true I'm writing primarily to a 50+ year-old white male — but he's got Black, Hispanic and Asian friends — and a wife or significant other. They're also buying the product as a secondary market. I don't want to leave them out!

Don't Forget... This Is Still YOUR Package

Once I get the final design back and I am OK with it, then I will give approval to the designer to go ahead and submit the file to the client. I get copied on that email and the designer lets the client know that this design is 'Carline-Approved' — meaning I'm taking responsibility for this baby!

The only time I've gotten really angry with a designer is when he's tried to circumvent this step of the process — either sending the design to the client without me seeing it or ignoring my crits and sending it anyway.

When that happens — and thankfully it doesn't happen often — I'm FUMING!

I will first let the client know the design was not approved by me. That usually hits the pause button on the project until I sign off on it. Then I'll go back to the designer and address the problem head on. I'll tell him point blank that we will not work together if he pulls a stunt like that again.

Bottom line: the copy does not go to the client until the copywriter says it's final.

There's only been one time in my 21 years as a freelance copywriter that I terminated a relationship with a designer for going behind my back to the client. He did it one too many times and I could no longer trust him. If I can't trust you — I can't work with you.

Top Designers, Top Controls!

I have a handful of designers that I love to work with. They're the ones I choose whenever I can. We've created some crazy and long-lasting controls. They get me. And since they're all so different — I've learned their particular styles so we can bring out the best in each other.

Now, if you're just starting out, you might be wondering how you're ever going to get an A-list designer to work on your packages... and the short answer is you probably won't. But then, you're not an A-level copywriter yet either. So it's OK to work with up-and-coming designers as you're also up-and-coming. Find one or two designers and start partnering with them.

If you don't know where to look — contact AWAI, Inc. (www.awaionline.com) — and start making connections.

The relationships I have with my designers have been built over 30 years. I worked with some of them even before I became a freelance copywriter. I am very grateful for these folks and all they've taught me.

I want to take this opportunity to introduce my top five designers who've made the most impact in my career — and show you a few of our Kick-Butt Controls...

Rob Davis is a Design Super Star!

My mentor, Clayton Makepeace, introduced me to Rob over 20 years ago. He told me, "This guy will take your copy to the top!" Clayton was not exaggerating.

Rob Davis

As a copywriting/design team, we are a force to be reckoned with! I often joke that Rob is me — in the design world — except he's a big-time introvert. But when he's designing — man, he really comes out of his shell! He takes my crazy headlines into another stratosphere!

I love that Rob knows how to subliminally engage readers in his design.

For example, when the reader is getting closer to the sale, Rob likes to put an image of the product on the bottom right of the page. That way, every time the reader turns the page — he has to touch the product!

When I write, I tell the reader what to do. When Rob designs — he SHOWS the reader what to do.

If he designs a quiz, he'll include a photo of a hand filling out the answer. He's putting the reader INTO the copy and showing him what we want him to do.

He walks the prospect through the process and he makes it easy, fun and enjoyable.

Rob and I have dozens and dozens of controls together. An iconic package was called *The Shocking Truth About Cholesterol Lowering Drugs*.

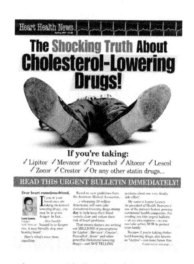

Man — the cover with the soles of the dead guy's shoes
was powerful!

This 'soles of the shoes' cover was a control for over four years.

One of our more recent packages was *How Not To Drop Dead.*

Ooh boy did this cover get people's attention!

I was tired of writing about how to live longer and decided to put a spin on it. Well, Rob took that headline and blew it out of the water! He had a businessman in a suit walking along the edge of a cliff and the water below was full of sharks. Each fin had a serious health problem written on it — and man, did that package get people's attention!

Oh, and when I got an offer to write copy for the German market, it was a no brainer — Rob was my guy! For the past few years, we've had some home run hitters — and lots of fun! Here's one of them…

Rob's cover with the German translation of my hard-hitting headline: "The Big Fat Lie Keeping Germans Sick, Dumb and Tired!"

* * *

Rick Thayne

Rick Thayne and I are polar opposites.

I can just visualize him bracing himself for our whirlwind conversations! He's a chilled-out, mild-mannered guy… who manages to WOW me with his designs!

Rick and I started working together over 15 years ago at Health Resources… then at True Health… and now at Peak Pure & Natural.

I can count on Rick to give me a solid package —

and then I PUSH him out of his comfort zone and challenge him to give me out-of-the-box test covers. And boy oh boy, does he deliver!

I've probably had more controls with Rick than any other designer. That's because we've created 10 to 12 promotions a year for over 15 years!

One of our first controls was for a chelation package, called *The New Chelation Miracle.*

He designed an iconic cover that tied into the story of soldiers who had gotten heavy metal poisoning from painting ships with lead paint.

This caused life-threatening issues with their hearts, lungs, memory — and the

Rick's iconic chelation package spoke to a generation of men who had served in the military.

only thing that saved them was chelation therapy.

Rick knows how to take the fears of the market and turn them into compelling covers.

That promo mailed for over five years! More recently, I wanted to take advantage of the toilet paper shortage that was happening from the COVID-19 pandemic. So for a colon product, I gave Rick the headline *Use Less Toilet Paper!* — and he designed a new cover that beat the current control!

Rick is my go-to guy when I want a solid 'bread and butter' package — he really gets what the 50+ year-old white male market responds to best!

* * *

Lori Haller is a very dynamic and explosive designer. I

have to be the calm one when we work together!

Lori really studies her use of color. Her sales pieces may look spontaneous but she's carefully thought out every design element.

Lori Haller

Lori is a very strong team player — she wants input and feedback throughout the process. She will not give up until we both LOVE the end result!

When I got the phone call to write a promo for Oprah — Lori was my designer of choice. I not only wanted a winner — but I wanted GIRL POWER on this project. And she delivered in spades!

Lori's kick-butt Oprah cover. It was a tough project but it was worth it!

Another one of our legacy packages was for a liver and kidney product for True Health.

I was concerned that my 50+ year-old white male market wasn't too interested in his liver — so Lori found a way to get his attention!

She created a design of a guy with a very beat-up face, with the headline: *"If you could see your overworked liver — here's how it might look…"*

*Lori really hit it out of the park with this 'liver guy'
cover!*

That package was unbeatable for over four years!

Nicole Mellott

Nicole Mellott and I go waaay back to our Phillips Publishing days. She was this young kid in the design department creating some really cool packages. It wasn't until years after I became a freelancer that I heard Nicole had also gone off on her own. I knew I wanted to work with her!

Nicole is fast — and she just GETS ME! One of our most famous packages really changed the way our market dealt with colon health. Before we came along, most covers talked about "poor bowel function" or "digestive distress."

But when Layne Lowery called and offered me the assignment to work on Advanced Colon Care II — I had to find a way to make this product stand out in the market. So I gave Nicole the headline, *Can't Go?*

This became one of my most successful packages ever.

Nicole found one of the most memorable photos I've ever seen on a package — a bald guy sitting on the toilet, straining to 'go'. When I saw the design, I thought, *"Man, let's cut out a lot of copy and let this photo say it all!"*

This cover test caused an uproar in list rentals. Some list owners thought their customers would be offended by the photo — so they actually refused to rent their names to be used on that cover! They finally came around when they saw other competitors allowing rentals.

That package mailed for nearly six years — and a lot of 'wannabes' knocked off this idea with their own version of guys straining on the toilet!

And one of those 'wannabes' was Layne Lowery himself. In addition to owning Health Resources, Layne also owned True Health, which had a similar product with slightly different ingredients. The *Can't Go?* package worked so well that Layne knew it was just a matter of time before other companies were going to follow suit.

He wanted to get ahead of them, so he asked me to write another colon package for True Health. I didn't have time in my schedule, so we came up with a Band-Aid solution: I would change the copy to include the new ingredients, change the headline to *Wanna Go?* and get Rick Thayne to redesign the package.

And guess what?

Wanna Go? was equally successful for many years! I never bothered to write a new promo — but I did get paid royalty checks for two packages instead of one!

In fact, both packages mailed until Layne sold the two companies. Those controls didn't fatigue — they retired!

And I gotta give Nicole the credit for that original *"Can't Go?"* cover design that kicked butt!

Recently — Nicole and I had some fun with a CBD product called Hemp Chucks. Her cover for *Joints Feel Stuck? Pop a Chuck!* gave me a new control!

The fun, fresh vibe of this cover captured the feeling of youth that our market was missing!

* * *

Larry Owen designed my very first blockbuster control with Clayton Makepeace. It was the infamous *Forbidden Secrets of Sex and Healing* package.

Larry Owen

This promo launched the very successful *Prescriptions for Healthy Living* newsletter.

Larry's cover spoke to men who wanted their mojo back!

Larry would often call me up and tell me about a client who had a great product and needed killer copy. Once he introduced me to the client — he and I became the creative team. And he really is an extremely creative person.

I joke with Larry that he's so emotional that when we work together, I feel like I'm the dude! But his emotion and passion about his work has given him a 40+ year career as a designer. We had another control that mailed for over five years for a chelation cream product — using a very long headline.

I've had the privilege to work with many, many other designers in my career — including the super talented Ted Kikoler during my Georgetown Publishing House years. Space doesn't allow me to list them all. By paying homage to my Fab Five — I am showing utmost respect for the designers who make copy come alive.

A great direct-response designer is worth his or her weight in gold and working with designers you trust and who give you lots of creative energy is a huge gift.

I couldn't do what I do without the amazing designers I get to work with every day. I truly believe that

Larry made my long headline readable and appealing.

all great copy packages are also great design packages.

TEN

You Ask, I Answer!

This chapter is here as a special thank you to my CopyStar readers. During the process of writing this book, I asked my e-zine readers to help me create a legacy book for them — and the new generation of copywriters — to get stronger at their craft. These folks are awesome! They've cheered and supported me throughout this entire process. They even voted on the design cover — so you can thank them (and Rob Davis) — for me popping out of the head of the 50+ year-old white male!

I've been answering their questions throughout this book. But I'm showcasing the following questions because I think they deserve more in-depth replies...

Question #1: How do I get high-paying clients?

Well, you don't start off getting high-paying clients. If you did, you would probably lose them. If you're starting off, you probably haven't honed your skills well enough to do battle with the big dogs in copywriting.

I would not recommend you finish a basic course and then start going after the high-paying clients. That's suicide! You've got to cut your teeth. You need experience.

If you have copywriting skills — and need clients — my #1 recommendation is to attend AWAI's copywriting seminars. This is the PRIMO place to meet clients who are actually looking to hire writers. I've seen so many careers blossom after attending the Job Fair at the annual AWAI Bootcamp in Delray Beach, Florida.

You'll also meet experienced writers who are willing to spend time talking with you — and who might even introduce you to some of their clients! You'll also get spec assignments you can take on and if the client likes your writing — you get paid! It's an awesome event and I look forward to it every year.

Although the 2020 Bootcamp was canceled because of the COVID-19 pandemic, the folks at AWAI will be back to hosting new Bootcamps whenever it's safe to attend. I'll tell you this: every time I attend a Bootcamp, I think it can't get any better. And every year I'm proven wrong!

AWAI also puts on different types of seminars throughout the year to target specific niches. So check them out! They're amazing opportunities to network... Network... NETWORK!

Most of my successes came from working with small companies who had good products... an ethical attitude... and who were open to trying new creative ideas. Help your clients grow to the level they want and they'll help you grow to the level you want!

Let me tell you a story. Back in 2005, Clayton started working with a company called Health Resources. He hadn't worked in the health market for several years. He was focusing exclusively on the financial market. But the owner, Layne Lowery, heard about Clayton's reputation and asked him to write a package. So Clayton called me for an update on what was trending in the health market.

We talked for a few hours and he said, "OK, I've got an idea for the package and if it works out, I'm going to need your help." Well, he gave the company a kick-butt control. A few months later, he called me up and said, "This client is great, but I don't have the time. They need a solid writer, so how about we do a joint partnership?"

We agreed that I would do most of the writing and he would copy chief the packages. So I met with Layne and his Health Resources team and we got started. Almost instantly, I was swamped with work — and I loved it! Our packages were kicking butt in the mail! It was a win-win-win. The client was getting controls. I had steady work. And Clayton didn't have to work too hard as a copy chief.

Layne was a brilliant marketer. He knew all the success he was experiencing meant there would be more competition in the market. And like I told you at the end of the last chapter, he decided to become his own competitor. He launched a sister company called True Health. And I just loved working with these companies.

After about two years, Clayton wasn't even checking my copy anymore. He was sending it directly to the client. But we were still splitting royalties 50-50. By this point, I realized this relationship needed to change. I finally got up the guts to tell Clayton I was finishing off the year under our agreement and then I was going solo. I braced myself for his response. But he just started laughing and said, "It took you long enough to figure out you didn't need me anymore!"

So, I started working directly with Health Resources and True Health and became their primary copywriter. It was an amazing experience to watch those businesses flourish. And my copywriting income was skyrocketing. That's no exaggeration...

Here's what Layne Lowery said:

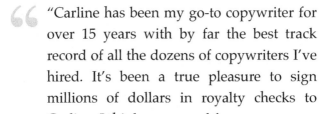

"Carline has been my go-to copywriter for over 15 years with by far the best track record of all the dozens of copywriters I've hired. It's been a true pleasure to sign millions of dollars in royalty checks to Carline. I think our record for one year was 14 new launch packages... exhausting!"

Layne eventually sold both companies, but a few

years later, he wanted to get back into the health space, so he got in touch with me again. This time, he and his business partner, Julie McManus, launched Peak Pure & Natural. And we're kicking even bigger butt with this company down to this day.

That's how you get the high-paying clients — you've gotta build the high-paying skills!

When you're getting started, find the clients who have big aspirations but who may not have the big budget yet. Show them what you can do! Create an opportunity where you both win from teamwork.

This works even if you've got very little experience. Remember how I used just ONE promotion to start getting more and more clients? You can do that too!

Take a look at your local mail. Who's sending out postcards, flyers and letter promotions? Target local businesses, such as lighting companies, landscapers, chiropractors, dentists… anyone using direct mail is fair game!

Offer to write copy that will beat the pants off their control. Tell them they only pay you if your promo wins! That way, you overcome the initial fee objection and you get your foot in the door. Instead of taking money up front, you can make it a win-win by setting up a royalty arrangement.

If they give you a shot and your copy works — they're probably going to give you more jobs. That's the beauty of this business: if you can produce great results, your client will hire you over and over again. You're now a proven asset to them.

This happens a lot. There are a lot of companies who need good writers, but they may not have the money yet to pay an A-list copywriter. And if you're an aspiring writer, you need to get the experience first and then the money will follow. So work together and you'll both get what you want!

Question #2: How can you trust that a client will pay royalties?

The short answer is: work with good people you trust. And if you get burned once, don't stick around for it to happen a second time.

Ready for the long answer?

I will give people the benefit of the doubt. I will trust someone until they show me I should do otherwise. I think people are generally kind and considerate and when I meet somebody for the first time, I don't want to be guarded and miss out on getting to know the person.

But I'm not naive. I have had situations where I trusted a client and they did not deserve that trust. And as soon as somebody shows me they don't deserve my trust — I cut them loose.

If I'm dealing with a client and I feel that they are not being fair to me, I will tell them that. If they're not willing to address my concerns, I drop them as a client. Yes, I could sue them (and I'd probably win!) but the time and the energy that would take up is so negative.

What am I fighting for — more money? Heck, I can

make more of that without having to deal with toxic people!

Instead, I just decide not to work with them anymore. Now the beauty of this industry is that everybody knows *everybody*. So if a client burns a copywriter by not paying royalties — word gets out. If I'm thinking of taking on a client I'm not familiar with, I'll often call up a few of my copywriting colleagues. If they ever say, "He doesn't pay his royalties," I'm going to pass on the client.

Like I said, this is a very small, tight-knit industry. We attend seminars together. We share stories. We self-regulate. I remember a mailer once saying that he went ahead and paid a copywriter — even though the copy was crappy — because he didn't want his company to be the topic of conversation at the next copywriter roundtable!

In my 21 years as a freelancer, I can remember only ONE time a client didn't pay me my royalties... and that guy went out of business. There were two other times where I suspected I wasn't paid my total royalties and I severed the relationship with both those companies.

Let me give you a specific way to determine the amount of royalties you're due from physical mailings. The post office gives mailers the quantities of pieces mailed. You can request that info from your client. Then you simply multiply the number of pieces mailed by your royalty percentage agreement. For example, if the postal mailing form shows 500,000 pieces mailed and your royalty agreement is 3 cents per piece of mail, then 500,000 x $0.03 = $15,000.

Now, I will tell you this: I've never requested the actual postal mailing form.

Instead, the client sends me their monthly mailing report showing the pieces mailed. Then they send me the royalty payment based on the mailing quantity from the report. That's pretty much the standard in the industry. If you don't trust that your client is giving you this information, then you shouldn't be working with that client at all.

Question #3: Are there any other red flags I should look out for when working with clients?

Remember that you became a freelancer to get out of the corporate crapola. Don't get sucked back into it!

If a client:

- Stresses you out…
- Prevents and stifles your creativity…
- Can't make final decisions…
- Makes unreasonable demands…
- Is verbally abusive…
- Consistently pays the bills late, or not at all…

Get rid of them STAT.

You are also allowed to part ways with clients simply because you don't like working with them. This doesn't happen to me often, but if I think *"Ugh"* when I say someone's name, I'm probably not going to work with him again.

If I'm not enjoying working on the project, I'm probably not going to do a good job on it. And life's too short! I want to work with people who GET my crazy writing style... who WANT out-of-the-box thinking... and who can afford to PAY for success. And it's a bonus if I really, really like them!

When I'm thinking about working with a new client, I will just talk to them and listen to what they say. You can get to know a lot about people just by asking simple questions. Remember 'John', who was so distrustful of his customers? Even asking a question as simple as "What's your guarantee?" was enough to highlight a big disconnect we would have had if we worked together. He thought his customers would rip him off if he offered a guarantee. But I believe a guarantee lets me know the company stands behind its products. The relationship was doomed before it could start.

I want to work with people who have respect, empathy and ethics when it comes to their customers. I don't want to put my 50+ year-old white male customer in harm's way. I'm his advocate. I want him to have access to great products from outstanding companies. And I want to protect him from shysters and low-down dirty conmen trying to rob him of his hard-earned money!

On the other hand, when you find a match — a really good client who keeps you busy and pays the bills on time — then spoil the heck out of him!

Those clients are like needles in a haystack — so hold on to 'em!

Deliver strong copy every time... beat your deadlines... offer additional services such as consulting, copy chiefing, or critiquing other packages... and TELL THEM you enjoy working with them and appreciate their business.

Question #4: If my ideal clients already have great copy — how can I get them to give me a shot?

Just because your ideal clients are already working with great copywriters — that does NOT mean there's not a seat for you at their table...

... Because it's not the writers that matter — it's the *ideas*!

Clients are always looking for new ways to market their products. If you can come to them with an idea no one has tried before, they may be very interested and give you a shot. There's no limit on how many writers a client should be using. A client should never say, "I have enough excellent writers and I don't need any more, thank you very much!"

No — if you're a good writer, a smart client needs to meet you.

But keep in mind that no client wants to lose money. Some of my clients will only work with A-list copywriters — no exceptions. They give the writer the assignment, the writer delivers it, the package goes through legal and the client mails it. They don't have time to micromanage and they're willing to pay big bucks when the copywriter delivers!

These are the types of people I want to work with. They know that I know what I'm doing and they just want me to *do it* and give them winners — so they can focus on running their business.

But other clients will be much more willing to take on less experienced copywriters because they can't pay as much. They've probably been writing their own copy up until now, so they'll have a feel for what works — and they tend to be more hands-on.

If that's who you're dealing with — expect crits about your copy. And expect it to go through many rounds of edits too. Don't take this personally. It is *very* expensive to test new direct mail packages, so the client is doing his best to hedge his bet — and get a winner from a young writer.

Sometimes a package just doesn't work. It may have been well-written — but the message just didn't resonate with the market. Trust me — I've had many packages that BOMBED!

And if that happens? Don't give up!

If the client is willing to give you a shot at reworking the package — try a different approach. You can lead with a story… or a 'new discovery'… a testimonial… or maybe an in-your-face, contrarian 'Why X won't work' angle. There are many ways to rework your promo!

Like Coach Kozak from my HASFIT workout says, "Those of you who think you can and those who think you can't are both right." It's all about your mindset. If you think you can't do it, you're right. Get out of here — go find a safe 9-to-5 job. If you say you can — then go try and get it done.

But no matter what you do, make sure you have some fun along the way!

Question #5: What sets you apart from other writers to become a true A-lister? It can't just be hard work!

Honestly, I think it's because I don't take myself seriously.

I realize that there are A LOT of folks who are way more talented and smarter than I am. So I don't compete or compare myself to them. I think about Kid #4 and I try to have fun. I'm always ready to push past the boundaries of what works.

I go into a project like a little kid, saying, "Ooh! What are we gonna do here? How can I make my client squirm?" I wanna see them with scrunched-up faces, cringing and saying, "Oooh Carline! We like it but we're scared!" I get that a lot — and I LOVE it!

From the very beginning of my marketing career, I've understood that I'm in the minority in this industry. I saw that during my 12 years working at Phillips Publishing. I didn't fit into any of the stereotypes in the industry. That actually became very liberating. Why? Because when you don't fit in — you must create your own path. You can build your own ladder to the top — without trying to climb someone else's! I'm not a white male copywriter and that's OK! In fact — it's pretty darn GREAT!

Remember that meeting at Phillips when I asked why there weren't people of color in our magalogs? The answer was that our market was 50+ year-old white males... but I wasn't satisfied with that.

Nobody in that room looked like me. Nobody had my background. And that drove me to push to find out why we weren't representing people like me in our promotions. My gut feeling even 30 years ago was that there were plenty of non-white people buying those products. They just weren't represented in our marketing. I knew that because that's been the case in our society when it comes to minorities for generations.

I know that marketing is based on stereotypes: "We appeal to yuppies in their 30s... Our target market is women in their 40s with children... Our core demographic is baby boomers looking to retire." I get it! But I also know great marketers TEST! Great marketers don't assume — they let their market confirm or deny.

That's why I'm a big proponent of cover tests when a client mails my package. Sometimes I'll give him three... five... seven... or even ten covers to test. Each cover focuses on different aspects of our 50+ year-old white male market. Honestly, I don't care which cover works — as long as one of them gives me a winner! But that cover test will tell us a lot about where our market is RIGHT NOW!

Another reason I've been successful is that I'm really good at keeping things simple. I'm not trying to impress my reader — I want to embrace him. I want to put my arms around him and have a heart-to-heart talk with him. Back in the early 2000s, I was invited to meet my client Frank Cawood & Associates in Peachtree City, Georgia. Frank was not a social guy and very seldom participated in copywriter visits. But I was told that he insisted on meeting me to ask just one question. He said, "You have consistently been beating our sales letters for several years. I don't have any other copy-writer with a track record that comes close to yours. What's your secret?"

I just smiled at Frank and said…

"I write to my mom."

English is my mom's second language. So if I write copy that she easily understands — I'm pretty sure my 50+ year-old white male market will understand it too. This forces me to take complicated thoughts and ideas — and make them understandable and DOABLE!

And finally, another reason I've been successful in my career is that I push boundaries A LOT. For exam-ple, a few years after we launched *Health & Healing*, we had a mega successful newsletter and the company was making a lot of money. But that was in the US and I wanted to see if we could make the product work in Canada. I figured, why not try? At least half the country speaks English! I got the go-ahead — and figured out how to get us into the Canadian marketplace. And you know what?

It worked like gangbusters! Although the Canadian market was smaller, we were able to charge more for the newsletter. It became a very successful profit center for the company. So then I thought, *"Hmmm… what about the UK? They speak English there too!"* So I found the vendors I needed to help us launch *Health & Healing International.* I was so excited about this test — I really worked my butt off convincing the company to give this idea a try. So I was eagerly awaiting the response. And you know what?

It bombed. I mean, the results stunk up the place!

(The only good thing that came out of that test was that I got to attend an international conference in England — and I took my mom along with me. I was finally able to fulfill the promise I made to take her to Europe!)

So did I give up? Heck no!

I swallowed my pride and pitched another idea to my bosses. There's a huge Hispanic population in the US — so I said, "Let's launch *Health & Healing…* en español!" And you know what?

It worked! And it also became a successful profit center for the company for many years!

So do you see what I'm trying to say?

Don't be afraid to try. Great ideas come from asking simple questions: "What if? How come? Why not? Can we test it?"

Not everything will work — and that's OK. But you've got to try! I'm always ready to put my hand up to say "Yes, I can do it!" And then I have to go off and figure out how the heck I'm going to do it! I think it's a superpower!

If there's a successful package I'm competing against, I'll dissect it to try to figure out what the writer is doing. I want to know what I'm competing against. As soon as I've figured out what made the package work — I'm going to look for a new angle. I'm gonna try something crazy different. I have to, because if I go the same direction as that other writer, I'm probably not going to beat him. I gotta bring something new and different to my package to give me a fighting chance to get a control!

I once had a client call me with what he thought was great news. We had just got results back from the sixth package I wrote for him. He called to say he's never worked with a writer who has written six consecutive controls for his company. He was thrilled.

I was disappointed.

Sure — a 100% success rate LOOKS good — but to me, it tells me I'm playing it too safe! I told the client we need to get more aggressive with our testing. If everything is working, we're not pushing out of our comfort zone — and that's not me! I'm thrilled with an 80% success rate. Why? Because that means some stuff didn't work. And that's good! It means I was aggressive in the market. I tested new and different ideas. I pushed the client out of his comfort zone. And some of the ideas didn't work — and that's just the market setting new boundaries for me to push at a later time!

I want to keep swinging and swinging and swinging until I knock that sucker out of the ball park with a blockbuster control!

So don't get comfortable with success. Don't hold on to it too tight — because you won't take chances. And if you're not taking chances — you're not growing your business… your career… or your life. I took a chance on January 1, 1999 to hang out my copywriting shingle.

Best decision ever.

ELEVEN

Success On YOUR Terms!

W hen my kids were little, I had a sign on my office door that read:
DO NOT BOTHER ME UNLESS YOU ARE BLEEDING.

When they got older, I added…
FROM THE EYE!

I'd tell them point blank: "Your father is home and he's a trained emergency medical technician and fire-fighter. There is nothing he can't handle. Don't come downstairs screaming about your sister hitting you! Don't show me your cuts and bruises! Don't come down here at all!"

I had to guard my time.

My kids always came first, but on the days I was working and Mick was home, I had to focus on work!

Man, was it hard. I'd hear all this noise upstairs with the kids and I wanted to know what was going on, but I would tell myself, *"Don't do it! Mick is taking care of it!"*

If I went upstairs, there was an 80% chance my workday would end. I would get caught up, jump into 'mommy mode' and that would be it. Because I know I'm easily distracted — I had to learn to fiercely protect my writing time.

And that's still true more than 20 years later! Those three or four hours of morning writing time are when I earn my money.

If I give up that time, I'm giving up income. But once it's 2pm or 3pm — Momma's home!

This comes down to knowing what your personal priorities are — and sticking to 'em, no matter what (or who) tries to get in the way!

I knew there were a few things I HAD to do if I was going to be successful in my new business.

Put Your Priorities In Order!

I believe you can have it all — just not at the same time.

Mick and I started having kids at 23. I was glad to be young enough to be able to play with them and do the things I couldn't do in my childhood. I wanted to have my second childhood with my kids!

Now, I thought we would wait a few years — but six weeks after we got married, I was pregnant! So while my friends were pursuing career goals… volunteering to work in foreign fields… and enjoying life as couples — I was now a stay-at-home mom pulling all-nighters, breastfeeding and changing diapers.

I was happy for my friends and their lives. And I

was happy to have my kids — but those years were rough! I had become a wife and mother in one year — and I wasn't really sure who I was!

But Mick and I had agreed *we* wanted to raise our family — not daycare centers or babysitters. Our family was our priority. So while my friends were spending their early 20s focusing on jobs, travel and volunteer work, Mick and I were raising our kids. And then, this switch happened. Ten years later, my friends were having babies — pulling all-nighters, breastfeeding and changing diapers and I was the one working at a cool job, traveling and doing volunteer work.

Am I saying that one way is better than the other? Absolutely not. Am I dogging daycare centers and babysitters? No way. I'm just saying you have to decide what you want and set your priorities accordingly.

Like I said earlier, I believe you can have it all — just not at the same time.

Focus On What Really Matters

I have a sticky note right in front of my computer that reminds me of my core values: JOY, which stands for Jehovah, Others, Yourself.

My spirituality has got to come first because it centers me. It determines how I behave — the way I treat others is a reflection of how I view my relationship with my God. I know how He wants me to be. I know He is love. I know He expects me to act in harmony with my beliefs. And I want Him to be proud of me.

Then I focus on others. I look for ways I can be of service to other people. If your fist is closed, you can't accept anything. But if you open your hand, then you can give *and* receive. It's always about your friends, your family members, your neighbors — how can you help them?

Then it's time for myself. I try to take good care of the physical vessel I've been given. I make sure I exercise and I eat right because I know what a gift it is to have my health.

If I don't take care of myself and I develop a lifestyle-based disease, then it's my fault. And I'm not OK with that. But if I do the best that I can and take care of my health — and I still develop a lifestyle-based disease — then I blame it on sin and imperfection. I'm OK with that.

I make sure to do the things that make me feel good, that bring me joy, like traveling and hanging out with my friends, playing with my grandkids — all of that stuff nourishes and energizes me — and keeps me going!

When a big decision has to be made, I can use the JOY mentality to help me decide what I'm going to do. Is it loving of me to do this? Does this reflect the kind of person I want to be? Are others going to benefit from this? Does this align with my priorities and values?

And it's not just a matter of using your core values for your personal life — no. It's good for your career. It's good for strangers you meet. It's good for just about every situation you find yourself in. Life becomes very easy because it's very simple. If I wouldn't want someone to treat me like that, I'm not going to do it to them. I don't care who it is. You deserve respect from me.

Your Turn!

OK — so enough about me. It's your turn now. You've spent time reading this book. What are you going to do about what you've learned?

Are you going to go after your dreams — or sit on the sidelines?

Are you going to be brave and test out a crazy idea for a cover test or theme for a new sales promo?

Are you ready to launch an idea... a business... a venture?

To paraphrase one of my successful colon controls: "Just DOO it!"

Let me help you…

Take a few minutes to make your own list of priorities... dreams… and goals. Don't overthink it. We're in the Internet age, you can try anything! And the COVID-19 pandemic showed us that we can all create our 'New Normal.'

So what do you want to do?

I spent 14 years working for companies, hoping every year to get a raise or maybe even a promotion. And while I learned a lot, I never saw the exponential growth that I experienced when I became a freelancer.

Believe me: you don't have to know a whole lot, you

just have to know enough to get started. You can pay your dues working with small clients early on and as you get better, you can leverage your early results to get bigger and bigger clients. Even if it's slow going, you're still working for yourself and you're building up your freedom (and your ability to earn) every day!

And if you don't know what you're doing, find a course, find a control to study and just try!

If it doesn't work, you didn't really fail; you just learned what not to do.

I'm still trying new things right now. I'm launching different programs, courses and training materials (head on over to www.carlinecole.com and get on my CopyStar mailing list so you hear about these when they launch). Some of them may not work — and that's OK! I'll learn!

But I know that lots of things WILL work — because that's what happens when you take a risk and TRY.

And I'm excited to teach what I know and make sure that other people get to share in my success.

That's what I like.

All the stuff, all the money, that's not what matters. That's not what success is. That could all go away in an instant.

Being successful is having great relationships with the people in your life and being able to choose how you spend your time.

What matters is the integrity you bring to each day and using the gifts you have to show how much you appreciate them. It's about finding the joy in your life, having fun every day and trusting yourself to keep moving forward.

Being successful is about choosing what's important to you and going after it with determination and creativity. I hope this book about my experience will help you find success on your terms.

The 50+ year-old white male market gave me a phenomenal career in direct-response copywriting. I've been the voice of cutting-edge doctors and leading experts in the natural health field including...

- Dr. James Balch
- Frank Cawood
- Dr. Richard Couey
- Dr. Michael Cutler
- Dr. Derrick DeSilva
- Donald Elgie
- Dr. Dicqie Fuller-Looney
- Nan Kathryn Fuchs
- Dr. Scot Gray
- Dr. Allen Green
- Dr. Reinhard Hittich
- Dr. Jack Isler
- Dr. Susan Lark
- Dr. Marcus Laux
- Dr. Alex Livshin
- Layne Lowery
- Dr. Matthias Maas
- Warren Matthews
- Dr. Philippe Moser

- Dr. David Nelson
- Dr. Joseph Pergolizzi
- Rick Popowitz
- Dr. Stephen Sinatra
- Dr. Greg Smith
- Dr. Wayne Stevens
- Virginia Tims-Lawson
- Dr. David Williams
- Dr. Julian Whitaker
- Dr. Richard Wurtman
- Dr. Yan Ping Xu
- And many more!

For that privilege and honor, to serve this 50+ year-old white male market — which has thankfully expanded to include women and people of color — this mixed-race woman who stumbled into this crazy and fun industry and succeeded, humbly and respectfully says...

... Thanks Boo!

Acknowledgments

Oh my goodness, there are SO many people I want to thank!

(Just imagine me in a glitzy gown on a stage, tears flowing down my cheeks ever so gently and holding a bouquet of red roses in my arms!)

I would not be here today if it wasn't for the generosity and trust from industry leaders like Tom Phillips and Bob King. These men taught me valuable and powerful lessons about the 50+ year-old white male direct-response market. They made colleagues feel like family and encouraged me to develop my entrepreneurial spirit. I'm grateful to this day to both of them for giving me my entry into this crazy biz.

I'm thankful that Customer Service Manager Anne Marcelino was willing to give me a flexible customer service, $8 per hour, part-time job that became the birth of my 35+ year career in direct-response marketing.

Phillips Publishing was my on-the-job training in

direct marketing. And I worked with some of the best marketing and creative folks in the industry. Launching *Dr. Julian Whitaker's Health & Healing* newsletter created a revolution in the alternative health industry. And I can't believe I got to be there from day one.

During this journey, I am very thankful for the mentors and colleagues who taught me so much about the industry. They include: Tom Phillips, Bob King, Marshall Hamilton, Richard Stanton-Jones, David Franke, Lorna Newman Berry, Wendy Marsh Makepeace, Annette Payne, Erica Beyer Bullard, Sue Tomasso, Julie Noble, Kim Krause Schwalm, Martha Seitchek Patterson, Mardith Byer, Jill Goodenow, George Clemes, Jennifer Gaillard, Mary Highley, Jill Eisgrau, Nancy Cathey, Cindy Butehorn, Belinda Brewster, Tom Callahan, Brendan Talty, Kelly Cleary, Annette Moore, Mac Ross, Dave Bishop, John Farley, Vanessa and Ernest Henderson, Linda Rezven, Cindy Champion, Alyson Krogh, Pat Cotta, Gary and Karen Alexander, Jackie Briganti and so many more amazing folks. I'm sorry if I left your name out!

I also worked with many marketers and vendors who supported the company's growth and taught me some tremendous lessons along the way. They include folks like Susan Nabinger, Brian Kurtz, Michael Fishman, Vince Zamaria, Michael Troy and many others.

A HUGE thanks to my Cole Marketing $olutions, Inc clients who make every day a FUN day. These folks allowed me to take major creative risks — on their dime — even when they weren't too comfortable with my crazy approaches. They include: Layne Lowery of Health Resources, True Health and Peak Pure & Natural; Julie McManus (a.k.a. Virginia Tims-Lawson) of Peak Pure & Natural; Rob Riess of Nutricel; Caleb O'Dowd of Biscayne Labs; Michele Wolk of Boardroom; Dr. Reinhard Hittich, Peter Kaminiski, Sven Lueckerath, Olaf Janssen and Svenja Strmiska of Dr. Hittich Gesundheits-Mittel; Daureen Papinchak of North American Nutraceuticals; Rick Popowitz of Biocentric Health; Ashley Delaney, Sandy Haynes and Gail Clanton of Healthy Directions; Vic Di Criscio of Nordic Clinical; Martin Weiss of Weiss Research and so many others.

Thanks to Ken Carroll and Bette Schantz at Indegris-Design for keeping me relevant on the web. You make me look good in cyberspace.

A special group hug to the team at AWAI. You ladies ROCK! Thanks for bringing a much-needed avenue to help young writers succeed in this industry. And thank you for helping me create programs like, *"How to Write Health Copy Carline Anglade-Cole's CRAZY Way"* to help guide the next generation of copywriters: Katie Yeakle, Rebecca Matter, Denise Ford, Jade Trueblood, Helen Buttery, Jaclyn Mehler, Jill Perri, Sandy Franks, Francesca Tignor — and the rest of the amazingly talented staff!

To Clayton Makepeace, the BEST! I still have a difficult time putting "the late" before his name. If I had known how important Clayton would be to my career and my life, I would've recorded and documented EVERY meeting — EVERY time we spoke. My one regret is I procrastinated too long to write this book. I would've loved for Clayton to read it. I think he would have been proud.

And I'm thankful for Clayton's wife and my friend, Wendy, who will continue his legacy for future copywriters.

And speaking of this book — I've been wanting to write it for years. All the ideas and chapters were rattling around in my head. But it took attending Brian Kurtz's Master Class on November 11, 2019 to put things in motion. During my speaking session, I jokingly mentioned that if I ever wrote a book, I would call it, *My Life as a 50+ Year-Old White Male*. But I was busy being a working copywriter and didn't have the time to become a book author, too. Later that day, I talked with one of the attendees at the seminar. She was a writer and editor named Laura Gale. Laura said she could help me make the book happen. We spent months on weekly Zoom calls where I would talk out every chapter. Laura took those hours of conversation and organized this book. So without Laura's help, I would have my title but this book would be nothing but blank pages. So, thank you Laura.

A great big thanks to my in-laws, Melvin and Judith Thomas a.k.a. "Mommie-Love and Grandpa" for raising such an amazing son. Seeing the relationship between Mick and Melvin convinces me that Nurture can override Nature. They could not be more similar than if they were biologically related. Melvin — you are a classy dude. At 95, you can still turn on the charm.

And thanks, Mommie Love, for all the great times playing Scrabble in your kitchen… feeding us…and loving your grandkids!

To my big sister Vivian Toussaint Whaley — I'm sorry for stealing your clothes and making it seem like you were losing your mind. Your stuff was just cooler than mine. I was just trying to be like you. And thanks for sharing your swimsuit — and ocean time — at the one and only time I ever remember us going to the beach as kids. I also appreciate you giving me a nephew, Jason with a wonderful wife, Ebony. And letting me be "Favorite Aunt" to my niece, Jennifer.

And my little brother Gregory Anglade — I didn't mean to torment you — I just wanted you to be tough since you were the only boy with sisters and female cousins. I love you Greggy-Poo and I deserved that black eye.

To Mrs. Gwendolyn Hall who took me under her wings. After school, at the Rec Center at Keene Elementary School, you taught me how to crochet, play ping pong and enjoy crafts. You kept me out of trouble. You didn't have to…. you wanted to. I am very grateful for that. And thank you for introducing this little Haitian girl to "SI-rup" and pancakes.

To Estelle Greenfield for helping me get my first real office job at Delon Hampton & Associates. First time I ever worked in Corporate America — and for a black-owned company to boot! And an extra special thanks to Delon for sponsoring me in the 'Miss United Teenager'

Pageant. I wouldn't have won 'Miss Photogenic' if it wasn't for you!

Thanks to Jon Abbett, Marilynn Corcoran, Harold Painter and Todd Bathgate — my number-crunchers who help me fund my dreams.

Gotta thank my girlfriends — my homies (and their hubbies) — who have been with me through thick and thin.

I'm talking about my friend Denise Owens (Anthony): when I told her I was taking the copywriting leap — Denise said, *"Girlllll... are you serious? That's awesome — you can do it! And I've got some food in my freezer if you run low!"*

My sister-in-law Crystal Cole Martin (Horace) — who is my polar opposite. It's amazing how we can tackle a problem from completely different views yet end up with the same solution! I love having you as my sounding board. Thanks for being a terrific 'Aunt Crys' to my kids.

Tami (and John) Nelson — my children's "second parents". What amazing experiences we've had traveling around the world with "Aunt Tami" and "Uncle Johnny"!

Maria Herrera-Brown (Ronnie) — when we've shared maternity clothes, baby clothes — and even underwear — can we ever NOT be friends? Thanks for giving my kids four lifelong playmates: Mikhail, Skyler, Giovanni and Chayene.

Lori A-S Cloud — my Nicholas Orem Junior High friend who's popped in and out of my life for decades

— and I love it!

Miriam Saccomani (John) — the "Ethel" to my "Lucy" — oh, the shenanigans our directionally-challenged selves have gotten into... Shannon Breneman (Jason), my former assistant and provider of photo testimonials of gross illnesses for my promos. I'm glad you abandoned me to serve in a foreign field...

... Ursula King a.k.a. "Lil Ur" (Darrell) — I want you right next to me if we ever have to go into battle — and Darrell King — you are my Plus One if I ever get to meet Oprah!

Debbie Brown Grooms — thanks for helping me make the Pom Poms at Northwestern High School and becoming my spiritual sister for life!

Cynthia Paschal-Hill (Ainsley) and Suzette Paschal-Crimson (Joel) — I can never trust either of you when you say you're staying for just a *few* days. You have practically lived with us for years. And Cindi — our Dr. Oz experience was DA BOMB! Love seeing you grow into a fellow copywriter.

Roz — a.k.a. "Woz" Roscoe (Nat) — my spiritual daughter and friend with an amazing memory and voice. You forget NOTHING!

Terri Tyler Landrum (Bobby) — you just showed up one day and told me we were going to be friends — and you were right! Who does that? YOU — that's who!

Maria Charagh — who took the plunge and ditched her energy-draining job to become the 'German Carline.' You make me sound so smart — Danke schön!

Sherrie Burgess-Brooks (Barry), who provided me

with a home-away-from-home in college — and has remained in my life ever since. Thanks for sharing your parents Leroy and Rosemary with me. The opportunity you gave me to spend a day with Sidney Poitier was AWESOME — thank you!

My spiritual moms Sally Castion (George) and Cynthia Epps (Kevin) — you molded me in the BEST way ever.

And to my cousin and spiritual sister, Sandy Ferguson (Marlon): I love you to the MOON and back!

My International Brotherhood of Jehovah's Witnesses is unlike anything else in this world. I'm so thankful to be a part of this spiritual family. Oh, the places I've been and the people I have met! To know that I can travel anywhere on this entire planet and all I have to do to be with family is find a Kingdom Hall of Jehovah's Witnesses — that is priceless. The love, friendships and unified bond keeps me grounded and gives me a powerful hope for an amazing Paradise to come. It also reminds me that no matter how wonderful my life may be right now — the BEST is yet to come.

And to my husband, children and grandchildren. I've talked about you throughout this book — so I just have three short, simple words to sum it all up: I Love You!

And last but *never* least, I thank my God, Jehovah, for the blessings... the people in my life... and the promises that will become realities in the very near future.

www.jw.org

Now, before you go, I have one more thing for you. As a way to thank you for reading this book, I have a gift for (and it's pretty awesome, if I do say so myself).

Turn the page to find out what it is!

That's Not All, Folks!

Did you think that was it? No way! We're just getting started on our journey together... and I want to give you a gift (well... 17 gifts, to be exact) to show just how committed I am to our relationship.

When you follow the link on the next page, you'll be taken to a special page on my website. On that page you will find a downloadable copy of EVERY SINGLE ONE of the controls we've talked about in this book.

Yep — I'm giving you full access to 17 of my most successful controls — for FREE! That's a value of over $850... and the education you'll receive from studying them is priceless.

There are controls for all kinds of products — from joint pain, to digestive health, to overall circulation... and you'll even get that famous Oprah package!

Now... when you download your free gifts, will you do me a favor?

I want you to study the heck out of 'em! Use them to make yourself a better writer.

You might be wondering why on EARTH I would give away my valuable 'insider knowledge' about what makes kick-butt health copy — but there's a method to my madness.

See, if I tell you my secrets, show you my winning packages and reveal powerful lessons learned — then you're going to be empowered to write killer copy for the health market, too.

That means I've gotta keep growing and coming up with even more crazy and better ideas to stay ahead in this industry.

If I'm training my own competition, it's on me to keep innovating! That's exactly what I want to do… and I want you to be there for the ride!

Just go to carlinecole.com/mylifegifts to get them all. Just enter your details to receive your FREE promos!

OK — don't forget to save your free gifts somewhere you can access them easily and print them out to study them! Then when you have an "Aha!" moment, email me! I'm at carline@carlinecole.com — I want to hear from you so I know that you're making your way towards the life and career you've been dreaming of.

Now… time to go make the dream a reality! Download your gifts and I'll look forward to hearing from you.

Made in the USA
Middletown, DE
16 September 2020

19987029R00136